PasT 7.

W9-ACQ-687

BLESSED IS THE PEACE

OF MY CHURCH

by
Yves Congar, O.P.

DIMENSION BOOKS
Denville, New Jersey

CARMELITE MONASTERY
LIBRARY
SARANAC LAKE, N Y

262.52(21)
Cob

First English Edition
Published by Dimension Books, Inc.
Denville, New Jersey
1973

Imprimi potest: N. Rettenbach
                      Pri. Prov., Paris

Imprimatur: E. Berrar
                      V.E., Paris

Copyright © DIMENSION BOOKS, INC.
All rights reserved.

Translated from the French by Salvator Attanasio.

TABLE OF CONTENTS

The problems posed by the present position of the Church are infinitely more profound and vast than those which we treat of here. These massive problems we do not even pretend to solve. Still, a person of my age who has worked a great deal for the Church and given her his best for several generations and who is still making an effort to understand the new questions may justifiably be allowed to make a contribution to the fund of common reflection available now — a contribution born of experience but necessarily connected with its traditional patterns of analysis and with its familiar references. I have known the Church at rest, I have grown up in her days of peace. Those who arrive at personal responsibility in a Church in motion and who have known nothing else obviously have a keener and, perhaps, more impatient awareness of the changes to be wrought. This is a privilege, to be sure, but only up to a certain point. For a movement is not a renewal of the Church unless it maintains a continuity with the Church of always. The contribution of this book may also be successful insofar as it suggests a need for a friction-less, rupture-less transition.

At stake is the fruitfulness of the work of the Council in the generation to come. We see quite clearly how certain undertakings born of impatience, certain ill-grounded or insufficiently verified initiatives could compromise its achievements. Those who make the Council itself responsible for these exaggerations are in error. It is not from the work of the Council that certain arguments draw their inspiration — an inspiration which, at times, is even at variance with it: producing divisions which lead to and, at times, deliberately set their sights on demolition and devastation. Growing numbers of the faithful are alarmed over initiatives and remarks whose provocative character, at times, is exaggerated by publicity. Catholics should understand that many questions, even those that may trouble them, are not posed merely for the pleasure of changing and of criticizing, but proceed from serious data and real needs. They must try to understand these questions and cooperate in finding a solution to them. We cannot seek refuge in resignation. For this would indeed be tantamount to a verification of the alarming formula: "We are a Church of yesterday in a world of today."[1] But at the same time we Catholics must reassure ourselves that we are not alone in believing that our Church, while it is the Church of today and prepares itself to be the Church of tomorrow, remains the Church of always. This is the meaning of the Council, and this is also the will of the most lucid and perceptive among the leaders of the Church today.

Fr. Yves Congar

One

A CHURCH IN THE MIDST OF TROUBLE

My deepest conviction is that the Church, in addition to her many other functions and resources, is a maternal hearth. This is a fact recognized through the centuries by the greatest number of those who appreciated the meaning of the Church in history. But beyond this, the Church is not only a mystic reality and a spiritual hearth; she is made up of human beings, and therefore she exists according to certain inherited forms of history; she is engaged in this history in which she shows a certain face and, consciously or not, conducts an appropriate political and social activity. A monk can live in the ideal Church without too much concern for the social action of the Church; but a lay person or pastor or sister laboring on behalf of humanity in the ghetto, for example, is necessarily confronted with the face that this Church shows to their world.

Without claiming to exhaust the subject, we shall distinguish four or five different attitudes which, in the whole of Catholic Christianity, represent various categories of people vis-a-vis the Church today.

A great number of Catholics simply do not pose any particular problem to themselves in their dealings with the Church. They may experience this or that particular general inconvenience, but they follow the main body of the flock and they accept, perhaps with a bit of grumbling now and then, their pastors as they are.

Others — perhaps ten percent of practicing Catholics — are deeply attracted to the mystic life of the Church and would like it to be made accessible to them in the forms to which they are accustomed. On the other hand, they are ill at ease with what they call the new orientations of the young clergy, of publications and of theologians. For some, the bishops, the Pope himself, appear to connive with the innovators. The latter appear to be preaching sociology instead of talking of God, of sin and of grace. And what a sociology! That of socialism, even of Marxism — and in demogogic tones that frown upon everything that represents the established order.

Many Catholics, whose numbers are difficult to determine but who represent the solid and vital center of the Church because of their dynamism and creativity, likewise prize the life of grace, the spirit of evangelism, the thirst for spirituality and communitarian concerns which they find in it. But they consider that many of its structures are superannuated and that, far from serving the Gospel, they constitute a hindrance to it. Moreover, these structures, they feel, markedly brake the advancement and liberation of mankind. They suffer deeply because it is not the Church which leads the movement for human liberation. They look upon the Church they love and they see that this Church, when it was not forced to accept changes wrought without her participation — changes which more often evoked her opposition — an opposition of the power structure, the "gross animal" of which Simone Weil spoke and which she challenged — is concretely a force of social conservatism, that is to say, a force defending the established class. The Church is not interested in freedom, in the social struggle save when she herself is affected in the person of her ecclesiastics. The Church believes herself pure when she has preserved the freedom that is peculiar to *her,* even if the freedom of man is flouted. Consider the pontificate of Pius IX, the longest and one of the most important in history: he fought for his teaching authority, for his temporal power. But what did he understand, what did he have to say about the great problems that were clustering around him — the industrial revolution, the proletariat, colonialism, biblical criticism? As Newman noted at that very time, Pius IX was thinking of "Il Governo, Les Dirigeants," considering that if the government and the upper classes adhered to the directives of the "Church" (under this word, one was to understand a government) one would still hold onto the people .... For this purpose the Church under Pius IX bent its mighty efforts above all to develop new devotions, fresh observances and pilgrimages, while the needs of man at large were left to rot.

Is not what happened then repeating itself today, for example, in Latin America where the Church has had her chances during more than four centuries?

There exists a fourth category, its actual numbers still escape statistics but they are growing a little each day: Christians who see, or think they see, the certitudes of faith crumble under the multi-lateral

11

critique that strikes at them from several sides: the critique of Marx, Nietzsche, Freud, joined today by the structuralist analysis and certain theories of secularity. Those who are familiar with these processes of "reduction" wonder where one will be at in a few decades: Is this the beginning of the end?

Those whom Roustang has labelled as "Third Man" exist in the categories 2, 3 and 4 that we have distinguished, and probably also in a fifth category, made up of adult faithful who are attached to Christianity, even to the life of an ecclesial community, be it on the scale of a group of their own preference but who are increasingly beginning to exercise their own independence of judgment with regard to the teaching authority. As a rule, their independence is low-pitched in its tone: the vociferous contesters belong to the third category.

We could envisage things from the viewpoint of the responsible pastors, in particular from that of the Holy Father. He presides over the Church. He must plan out the harnessing of horses, some restive, others runaways. Admittedly, his is a difficult task. As co-responsible sons, we shall not try to increase his difficulties, even when we take account of them. Actually, this approach is very rare today; many are impatient and intolerant in their demands. It is from their viewpoint that we wish to consider the question. Facts are facts. It is useless to deny them, even if they are contrary to our views. It is better to know them and to recognize them. But they must be exactly established, in the difficult density of time and space and within the actual community of the people of God.

We speak of the density of time in order to include in it the future as well as the past. We judge in terms of the ideal, but things have a context. They are dated. We cannot expect men of another epoch to have acted according to our criteria of today. But often, by travelling over thousands of miles, we also travel over centuries. There are geographical as well as historical contexts. On the other hand, knowledge of the past allows one to enlarge one's ideas, to relativize judiciously one's evaluations. We see that many different ways of doing things have existed, we discover ideas concerning the Church and concerning other matters of theology, things much broader in scope than ones of the present day. Our own experience has proven to us that many intellectual difficulties can disappear when viewed within an historical framework. Assuredly, the majority of the faithful are to be excused for not having an historical perspective on things, but they must also recognize that they often lack the intellectual means to resolve the questions they pose. Most people have the grace or humility to do this today.

At any rate the future, which hope leads us to include in our thoughts, is within the reach of all. We do not have the right to despair of the Church simply because there are difficulties. The present situation already contains some seeds of hope, and therefore, we cannot afford to give up. Assuredly, some will object there is urgency today. "If only tomorrow you give thought to today's urgent needs, tomorrow's urgent needs will likewise be unmet!" All I can say in reply to this is that the seeds will always be there and that suffices for us to work in hope and trust. Nothing has ever been accomplished under other conditions.

Our concern to integrate the density of time in our vision lies in the fact that it permits us to give our Catholic faith dimensions which assume an effort to reform or to update it. A reform of course is not a revolution, because it respects continuity. Yet it is quite different from a restoration, because it does not try to re-establish simply what was *before.* If we had absolutely to conform to the present situation, there would never be any possibilities for reform in it. If I imagined something wholly different, it would not be the reform *of the Church.* The Catholic faith must be preserved but not a vapid faithfulness accorded only to the actual form of things.

To be truly alive, our faith must plunge itself fully into the present day situation of the people of God. We are not alone. We belong to a people that has been created by a positive initiative of God in society and in the history of man. This people is animated to its core by the Holy Spirit of God, but only according to the structure that God has given to it and according to the vocations and the challenges that He ceaselessly arouses in it: therefore, we must be attentive to one another, take account of one another, in the keen, intelligent and critical consciousness of what one is oneself and of what others are. Is not such a consciousness the decisive condition for true and sound behavior in any sphere? On the part of the faithful this will involve docile attention toward the teaching of the pastors but also, on the part of the latter, a very dedicated and selfless attention to what God offers them to understand through events and through the faithful. The school of the Holy Spirit is a school of simplicity, but not one of ease nor of simplism.

A very serious difficulty, one which weighs heavily upon the most committed of Christians, must still be discussed. It is not preeminently and absolutely what the Church says or thinks of her own role that is of first importance today. Such things can be self-serving. What counts in this post-Conciliar period is what the Church can say to the real questions posed *by the world;* even the questions concerning the Church.

Something profound and authentic is involved in this, but only up to a certain point, or under certain conditions (hence, not in an absolute manner). If, by pushing logic to the extreme, one were to understand, simply as a fact, that there is but one reality, man, and that Christ is but man perfected; one reality, the world, and that the Church is but service, we absolutely could not be in agreement. We should never cease to denounce a danger of deterioration of self-definition under the name of horizontalism or under any other name or one bearing no tag at all. The fact remains that one can, without making pretensions of this kind, pose to the Church not only the questions of the world but the questions of the service of the Church understood in terms of the needs of the world: it is the world which today dictates many conditions. That does not influence only matters of Justice and Peace and development

15

but even of ecclesiology itself. We admit that. But we must point out a new possible danger to the faithful and to the clergy alike. One risks nourishing oneself exclusively on the foods of the world. Today they are bountiful and, at times, heady. They are communicated to us in great profusion, often with such demanding shrillness through the radio, the press, technical and professional publications and even voices of Christian organizations. That is very good. But it is also necessary to regain a footing in the Church and in her spirituality insofar as she is the maternal hearth of which we have spoken. We must suitably feed on the nutriments of the Church — those of the communion of Saints, of the liturgy, or of silence before God. Otherwise, we shall all laicize ourselves in the pejorative sense of the word.

Our maternal hearth is there. Whatever certain persons may say, it is intact. We shall find our models there: an abundance of sound books and publications, the celebration of the Eucharist, possibilities of fraternal dialogue. And our hearth offers more than one room; there are rooms facing north or south, east or west. This does not mean to say that no difficult problems exist. But in the full consciousness of the limitations of our effort, we should grapple with them while God gives us strength and courage.

Two

SHALL WE DE-CLERGIFY THE PRIESTHOOD?

Troubles in the priesthood were perceptible and were voiced many years before the Council. During the Council itself priests had the impression, at times even to the point of anxiety, that they had been overlooked in the proceedings. The assembly had given thought to addressing a message to priests, and at least two drafts were drawn up for this purpose. Rather than offer generalities and exhortations, it was considered more helpful to tell priests who they are and to help them find their exact identities. This is what the Council tried to do in the decree *Presbyterorum Ordinis.* But have all priests read it? This document, though inevitably imperfect, represents an important effort at husbanding the resources of the Church and deliberately goes beyond the categories of the sacred and the cultic, at least taken in the strict sense: it places the priest in the apostolic category, and in close association with the bishops.

Nevertheless the malaise continues. And this malaise has been very exactly analyzed and defined: every man has the need to be "recognized" by other men for what he is, he has a need to be "received."[1] This is the pre-condition for his integration into the human community, without which he has the unbearable feeling, at least in the long run, of being a useless person, a parasite, an outcast, a pariah. This

analysis remains exact and enlightening. It has also
been pushed further. Analysts have not been content
merely to establish a lack of integration on the part
of priests, but have sought for its causes. Obviously,
there is the fact that the modern world is taken up
with its construction of the "secular" without paying
enough attention to eternity: "Dum nil perenne
cogitat," says the hymn of Sunday Vespers. Of what
use is a priest in a technologized, urbanized, social-
ized world? To celebrate some ceremonies? ("it's
only in church that one can conduct a ceremony
properly," an anti-clerical friend once said to me. But
that was twenty-three years ago, and it's no longer so
true). To spare parents the bother of taking care of
the kids? But this is precisely what priests do not
want people to take them for: baby-sitters. They
protest, not only in the name of their priesthood, but
in the name of their manly dignity, against this kind
of "recognition" which "receives" them only for an
illusory usefulness and one which is alien to the true
life of men.

The root of the malaise is to be sought deeper. If
there is no integration, which obviously calls into
question the exercise of the priest's mission, it's
because the priest misses first of all being a man
among men. He is prevented from achieving this by a
formation and by a clerical calling which place him in
a human world different from that of other men.[2] As
long as priests are placed under the obligation to
adopt a culture, a language, a way of life that are not
those of other men, there will only be lame solutions,
ineffective palliatives. Hence, it is necessary to de-
clericalize the priests, and even to de-clergify the

18

priesthood. Was this not something that the worker-priests, who were the advance guard of the church, had understood long ago? One of them quite recently recalled: "I said and I repeated to my religious Superiors that if we intended to remain priests, we should have to abandon forever the condition of clerics."[3]

But, then, speaking of the restrictive measures that had been imposed on him, he added: "The world was ready for Christian action, but the Church stood in my way."

There has been much written on this subject, but one of the most significant documents in France was a letter of 45, then 120, then 300, and finally of 526 priests who on January 11 and 12, 1968 held a meeting constituting as it were a priestly representational body before the episcopate.

The first signatories of this letter explained themselves clearly:

"Taking note that, in large, Jesus Christ has not been received in our world and that the indifference to Him is evident, our analysis forces us to believe that the clerical status imposed on priests, with the life-style and the mode of relations with other people that it involves, is one of the major obstacles to this revelation of Jesus Christ. In consequence, the rejection of the clerical status appears to us as a necessary pre-condition for defining our mission anew . . . ."

Instead of isolating themselves from other people, especially young persons who wish to respond to the call of Christ, instead of giving them a Church-stamped formation and mode of being, and then parachuting them into the mass of men to whom they will have become more or less strangers, they advocated leaving them in their milieu and having the Church entrust them there with a mission that could be definitive. They went on to say: "It (the rejection of the clerical status) depends above all upon *the initiative of the clerics themselves,* by a refusal on their part to perpetuate themselves as such. It is obvious, however, that it does not appertain to us to define the mission of the Church. That depends upon the Church (lay-persons, priests, bishops)." This last sentence is important: we shall have to weigh it carefully. Such a radical re-examination begets observations and deep questionings. For my part I shall propose some ideas in four sections, and I shall do so with the fraternal sincerity of a priest who is well aware of belonging to the world of clerics (and not ashamed of it) and to an older generation but one still entitled (and indeed obliged) to speak. Let us say that this is my form of service.

    1. *The Idea of a Functional Priesthood:*

    The priesthood is not a "career;" the priesthood is not a "trade." These assertions accord with the formal Catholic idea that "priestly responsibility is permanent." But today we sometimes encounter pronouncements of a kind that betray less assurance: the priesthood is viewed by some as purely functional. When I leave the altar, some priests seem to say, I am a Christian just like anyone else.

    Yet theology and even Dogma speak of a permanent priestly "character." This is more than just a way of expressing the permanent significance attributed to priestly ordination in the Church.[4] Historically, the idea of a stable and even indelible "character" was introduced by St. Augustine in order

20

to establish the independence of priestly actions from priestly saintliness and to relate all work of sanctification deriving from a priest's ministry to the work of Christ. True, the character of the Sacrament of Orders is not exactly the same as those of Baptism and Confirmation. These two sacraments establish the *being* of the Christian. Orders establishes a ministerial representation, it is a charism of function.[5]

This functional value does not abolish the ontological permanence of the Sacrament of Orders but it could rightly relativize its exercise. History, up to the twelfth Century, presents too many contrary facts for us not to admit a certain social, ecclesial and canonical conditioning of the application of the principle: "Thou art a priest forever."

We should affirm, then, in this context, that the priest is not a "super-Christian." It no less remains a fact that Orders is a consecration of the whole being which contributes to the individual a new conformation to Christ, the sole and sovereign Priest. It is not a function conferred through simple nomination or designation. St. Hippolytus clearly noted this in a careful study of the very language of ordination.[6] It is a function established in an original sacrament, that is to say, in an *act of God.* We can understand the reality and the profundity of this fact only in the perspective of an ecclesiology of the Mystical Body; viewing it in terms of a theology of "the People of God," no matter how authentic it may be, is not enough. Through the rite of ordination — which is not something unexpected like a monolith sprung up before us in the desert, but a considered action which consecrates the whole process through which we have responded to the call of Christ — the Lord places His mark upon us and takes possession of us in a particular way. This is what Pope Paul said in his conference with Lenten preachers on February 26, 1968: "The certitude of the original, irreversible and unutterable relation that binds us to Christ is what we call the priesthood. Priesthood is not simply a function in the Church, a service contributed to the community, it is a sacrament, an interior sanctification."

Special, prodigious powers are conferred upon the priest which qualify him to act in the name of Christ. This is why these powers give him a wholly special, indelible character which makes of him a living instrument of Christ and thus establishes between him and Christ a particular and inexhaustible relation of love: "I have called you friends" (John 15, 14). The spiritual life of the priest ought to be continually nourished by the consciousness of his ordination and by the choice of Christ which has fallen on him through love: "You did not choose me, but I chose you" (John 15, 16). His spiritual life would not waver between doubt and lukewarmness if he were to experience deeply this invitation to a confiding intimacy, this immanent will of Christ, this loving and powerful will to act through his lowly person which has become forever available to Him.

True, this consecration does not involve the so-called "clerical" state. Andre Manaranche has rightly noted that neither Jesus nor the Apostles were clerics. But they were integrally consecrated to the announcement of the Gospel and to the building of the Church. Manaranche's assertion does not diminish the importance of these exigencies. True, certain historical forms assumed by the ministerial priesthood can be called into question; but we cannot call into question the consecration of one's whole self to the apostolic work such as is proper to the priest. The latter should be carefully distinguished from some forms of sacerdotal status which are, in themselves, historical and therefore relative.

On this point we must make a very important observation. Nothing in the world exists except in an historical form: this is true of the sacraments, it is true of the Incarnation itself. This historical form is relative, hence in itself is subject to change. It may be that it even admits of many imperfections and blemishes. It is legitimate to want to reform it, but care must be taken not to compromise, even more important, not to eliminate the valid reality which the historical form poorly translates. It's the old story of throwing out the baby with the bath water. Accordingly, we should be mistrustful of any radicalism, of any iconoclastic haste, of any theories or views or of any ideology which strikes at the fundamentals of our faith.

2. *The Church and the World*

For more than fifteen years, a deep desire has manifested itself among clerics and young religious to rid themselves of that which distinguishes them and tends to separate them from other men — a deep desire to be what the Germans, in a compound word which is almost untranslatable, call "Mitmensch," i.e. *with* and *like* other men; like, for *be with*.

I can recognize that, posed thus, the problem

23

lies at the heart of the Church today.[7] We come upon it again and again in the analysis of the present situation of priests, sisters and religious. There is in it a positive datum to which we must indeed pay tribute. But I also say: Beware! On a fundamental level it challenges the very nature of the Church and of its mission. At stake is their *specificity*.

First of all, the Church. What is fundamentally at stake is that she is something different from the world, something different even from the setting forth of a spiritual truth or spiritual dimension for the world, although it is incumbent upon her to do just that: for the Redemption brings to a focal point and perfects the whole object of Creation. We must respect the tension between the Church and the world, while at the same time we must recognize the bond that unites them. It is not enough to define this tension as a "Gospel-world tension," one lived in the personal confrontation of a consciousness dedicated to Jesus Christ and also involved in the events of men to whom our co-humanity binds us. There is something else, something very authentic which must be added to it. The faith — the Christian faith to which believers have given themselves for thousands of years of agonized joy and joyful agony — is a faith of prophetic contestation of an unjust and un-brotherly world. Taken literally, it can lead to a revolutionary commitment. This obviously poses questions of a depth that we shall not touch upon here. We content ourselves only with the recognition that, in addition to standing alongside the world, the faith also stands at times over it and against it.

The Gospel and the Church cannot be separated,

much less set over against each other, but they are not identical. Concerning the Church, we claim for her the quality of an original reality by divine right and by public law. Obviously, this is something that in these days will occasion a pouting of lips, even a shrug of the shoulders — and, admittedly, the claim of the Church has sometimes led to intolerable abuses of power. No doubt some of these abuses arose from a theoretical ecclesiology, in particular that of the pontifical documents or the theologians of the papacy, which was largely conditioned by the centuries-old rivalry between Church and State and which led people to conceive of the Church as a power confronting another power. We are just now emerging from this juridicism with a rather political bent. At bottom, the Church is not purely herself save in a secular society whose secularity she truly recognizes. In this regard, the proceedings of Vatican II are consistent and significant. But whatever be the awkwardness that history permits us to perceive now, we cannot deny the validity and profound meaning in their own historical moment of various Papal protests through the centuries, from Gregory VII to Pius VII, from Gregory XVI to Pius XII, against claims either to vassalize the Church or to reduce religion to a sanctuary of the individual conscience. Given the limitations of history, this struggle was, and it remains, necessary.

What is at issue? Two facts that are closely connected: 1. The Church is the fruit of a series of divine initiatives that culminate in the Incarnation and in Pentecost, that is to say, the Mission of the Word and the Mission of the Spirit: events not reducible to the energies invested in Creation and giving birth to forces beyond human calculation. 2. These initiatives, and the fruit that proceeds from them, have a public character. This point is obvious; it is also very important. It explains the profound meaning of those historical signs that date from the great prophetic utterances during the Hebraic rule of kings.[8] By virtue of the fact that it has been the People of God, beneficiary of His revelation, the Jewish people has had and preserved, in an expressive fashion, its role as "a signal for the nations" of which Isaiah speaks (11, 12).[9] Its very existence attests the public character of the revelation which constituted it. Christ came likewise in an historical and public manner. The way in which St. Luke speaks (1, 5; 2, 1 ff; 3, 1 ff) recalls the historical character of the mission of the prophets. Christ did not come in some kind of diffuse presence and as if his existence were part of a general humanity: He made a public, obvious entry into human history − an entry with a universal and definitive meaning of which we are the witnesses and the ministers. The coming of the Spirit at Pentecost is of the same quality.

In more general terms, we might say: Christ is the sacrament of the love of the Father siding with our world to give it salvation, that is to say, the possibility of access to God beyond its own resources. The Church is the sacrament of this salvation, that is, the sign and the medium of this access to God. The two most precious ideas of the conciliar ecclesiology are the notions (1) of the People of God and (2) of the universal Sacrament of salvation. The bond between these two ideas is very close. One of the

26

important advantages of the "sacrament of salvation" is that it lends itself less to the abuse which has too often identified the Church with the hierarchy.[10] It is the whole People of God that hears the Lord and which is the instrument of grace. And in the light of the full ecclesial reality of the faithful, one can immediately perceive the exigencies incumbent upon the ministerial priesthood.

The whole People of God are marked by the sign of the Lord, but the priest, in dependence on the bishop, is more fully constitutive of it. From the point of view of preaching, as well as the celebration of the sacraments, especially the Eucharist which perfects the community in the Body of Christ, the episcopal and presbyteral priesthood binds us to the historical Incarnation through means positively and historically instituted for it. It is in this sense that the Council says that the priesthood represents Christ as the Head building up His body. And it is in this sense that H. Denis can speak of the priest as an "institutional person." This has important consequences. As an "institutional person," the ministerial priest will be supremely the man of the Church, the leader of the People of God, at whose disposition will be the totality of the instituted means of salvation, in dependence only on the historical Revelation and the grace of the Incarnation.

So, someone might say, "you wish to plunge us once again into the clerical state which all the present exigencies of the Church invite us to leave? If by "clerical state" is understood the cassock and the biretta, the seminary cut off from the world, an unctuous style and a language that nobody else

27

speaks, no, it is not a question of those things now. But if, by the clerical state, we understand the exigencies concretely necessary for being a man of prayer, a serious preacher of the word, an enlightened spiritual guide, a worthy liturgical celebrant, a man competent in that very thing that other men, believers and non-believers, expect from him, then, no matter what one may wish to call it — it is absolutely necessary. Its concrete forms can be varied but it devolves upon the community, under authority of its heads, to fix them and not upon the fantasy or frivolity of the uninformed. That is why, in our opinion, today's violent thirst for assimilation to the world greatly risks betraying those very values that make the Church something different from the world, and could lead to a loss of the feeling of tension that exists between the two.

The inverse error can also exist. That is the state of mind that creates sects and brings about divisions within the Church. The two contrary tendencies make up two families of opposed mentalities. The one pushes the logic of the "mitmensch" to the point of risking loss of the "asideness" of the Church, while the other lays stress on the "asideness" to the point of compromising the necessary "being with." Obviously, it is necessary to reject this unacceptable division and to preserve the tension, not only on the plane of a lived awareness but on the plane of the social and institutional sign which is the Church.

3. *The Mission of the Church*

For the Church, its mission is like the pupil of the eye: the means of her contemplation of the world and of herself. Some, proceeding incorrectly, want first to enter into the community of men through work, make this and all that it involves a necessary pre-condition of action by the Church and *then* re-define the mission for the whole Church: bishop, priests and faithful. Vatican II took the opposite approach: it first defined the mission of the Church, then it deduced the mode of life of priests and even their daily work on that basis. I am quite aware that this declaration was made after a careful analysis of the world situation and a frank recognition that certain steps were necessary if the Gospel were to be more present in mission lands. Nevertheless, I should like to make these observations here.

a.   Our epoch has enjoyed an extremely notable development in the human sciences: psychology, psychoanalysis, sociology, structural analysis, etc. What we need most today is not an anthropology of an ethical nature with suggested normative values, but rather techniques for understanding human behavior which may eventually furnish insights helpful to individuals and society. Very interesting possibilities may be hoped for in all these developments. But there is a tendency today to think of possibilities as if they were data pure and simple, and therefore normative, beyond debate and question. The theologian, who is duty-bound to criticize such simplistic theories is frequently rejected, at times in advance, as the representative of a vanished species, or one doomed to disappear shortly. Theologians are far from being beyond all reproach but, if they are faithful to their vocation and to the conditions of its valid exercise, they certainly have something worth listening to. On another level, the same goes for

29

responsible pastors. It is not up to the sociologist nor to the psychologist to dictate normative principles in spheres where such principles already exist, above all if they derive from positive Revelation. Therein lies the first and most imperative necessary pre-condition. We will never be too many in trying, all together, to recognize it, and to conform ourselves to it, while still taking account of fresh discoveries from new fields.

b. There exists another tendency whose limits of validity it is important to appreciate, because it is valid, but only up to a certain point: that of defining the mission of the Church, not through its origin and through the fact of being "sent by," but through its content, which is the communication of Jesus Christ, of His active love, of the meaning that He gives to life. It seems that for some the fact of spreading the Gospel, in one way or another, suffices to define the mission of the Church. Does not the conciliar decree on the apostolate of the laity itself operate thus, by identifying mission and apostolic activity (Nos. 2 and 23)? Yes, but perhaps it is valid in that case without expressing the whole truth of the situation.

There exists in fact, two definitions of mission, one broad, the other strict. There is the mission through responsibility of the gifts that one has received and of the good that one bears in oneself: in this sense, every Christian is responsible for spreading the Gospel and the charity of Christ. And there is the mission deriving from a formal mandate, namely, the one that Jesus Christ, as Envoy of the Father, communicated by an express injunction to His apostles: cf. John 10, 36; 17, 8; 20, 21; Mt. 28, 18-20; Mk 16, 15; Lk 24, 47-48; Acts 1, 8. Karl

Rahner has defined the apostolate of the laity in a famous article whose meaning accords perfectly with our reflection here:

"The hierarchical apostolate is constituted by a mission that *displaces* the apostle and creates the ministry; the apostolate of the laity, if it preserves the features that differentiate it from the hierarchical apostolate, is the apostolate of the man at the place that is his in the world. What determines the extension and the mode of this apostolate is not a particular mission received from on high, but a mission received from here below, that is to say, expressed by his situation in the world. The outline of its Christian influence is the very outline of its relations in the world. It does not have to be constituted there by a new mission and mandate."[11]

This is the place to recall a chapter of theology formulated in the nineteenth Century with an exemplary rigor by the school of the Roman College, in particular by Perrone and also in our days by Cardinal Journet or, in terms more purely biblical, by Fr. Dewailly, and on the plane of a full missionary witness by Jacques Dournes.[12] There exists an apostolic body, that is to say, a missionary body which forms a unique collective or moral person including Jesus Christ, the apostles, the body issued from them through an "apostolic succession," conceived not as the pure sacramental transmission of a power, but as the continuity of the mission with its envoy-authority, its content of faith or of message, its soul of grace and of charity. If one does not go as far as that, if one does not situate oneself as a priest in this missionary flow, inseparable from law and from love ("As thou Father didst send me into the world" of John 17, 18 is inseparable from "As the Father has loved me" of John 19, 9) one misses the main point of the matter. Generally, this question and others is approached in a too purely human manner. One should not institute any general debate that touches on it without first having re-read and meditated on the Lord's apostolic Testament contained in Chapters 13 to 17 of St. John.

The episcopal and presbyteral (and diaconal!) priesthood is situated in this indissolubly juridical and mystical structure, a structure of law and love, of institution and of spiritual happening — all of which are constitutive of the hierarchic mission. Men of little faith that we are, we go around the problem without going to the heart of it! Beginning with myself, I, who have the air of elaborating for others what they must do, I sometimes quite simply forget to just listen to what Jesus Christ says to us.

    c.   There is a further problem on the *content* of the apostolate. It is one that we have not personally encountered, but one which nonetheless clearly exists, as we can see from certain writings.[13] The problem concerns small groups of Christians scattered throughout the forms and structures of our secularized society, people who are not trying to "plant the Church," or to convert individuals, but only to make social groups more open to the creative action of God in them: for Christ acts *Incognito* in the processes of technology and of secularization, and thus Christian Messianism secretly builds a more human society.

Thus posed, the problem is the same as the one that we touched on under number 2. It boils down to a misunderstanding of the fact that the Church is a different thing from the world, that the history of salvation, although it unfolds in the history of the world and for it, cannot be reduced to common history; and that the Redemption, finally, cannot be reduced to Creation.

While this is not the radical problem we previously treated, it is invested in a situation where there is a certain aversion for the explicit announcement of salvation in Jesus Christ, at least in its classic form of preaching or even statement of the faith. The apostolate, as we see it, would consist principally in the confrontation of a Christian conscience with men and events. There can be a communication only through discussion of matters of trade, scientific research, love, the social or political struggle, etc. This way of viewing the matter is quite common today in the sphere of ecumenism.[14]

I do not think that this kind of apostolate is faulty, but that it is insufficient. Moreover, I fear that it runs risks of "temporizing" with matters of the faith, of dogma or of teaching authority. This risk would become dangerous if accommodations were turned into denials, or if adjustments for the sake of courtesy amounted to betrayal. Nevertheless simple presence can be a form of apostolate, and is susceptible of diverse intensities. Its plenitude depends on the degree to which one can communicate the Revelation of Christ. Its purity depends on the authenticity and transparence of Christ's presence through us, and its efficacy depends on the Spirit. And assuredly, the Spirit is not necessarily bound by our limitations.

4. *Priesthood as the sign of unity of the People of God*

As a priest, do I have the right to give another man a *valid* reason to consider me as his adversary — to the point where he could no longer speak to me, even if he had a spiritual need to do so? Here we have a real problem and a problem for which there are no easy or final answers. The clerical state (which, I repeat, does not necessarily involve the cassock and the biretta!) is the effective means of a certain transcendance and is in itself a condition or means of unity for all the People of God. I am not ignorant of the criticism people offer "purely religious" theories and positions so far above the fray, of how intolerable it is to invite others to get themselves wet while remaining dry oneself. But what are we to say of the danger inherent in priests taking positions that are entirely partisan or solely on the plane of politics? "We want to express ourselves freely, to take political, trade union or other options or commitments." One hears this everywhere today. Who does not see that a priest who does this runs the danger of being carried away or absorbed to the point of dividing Christians among themselves. We may have to live with this danger. But let us hope that the priesthood will never cease to be a sign of the unity of God's people.

Three

THE UNITY OF THE PEOPLE OF GOD

The unity of the Church as an idea or as a dogma is not at issue here; in a profound sense, it is something that can never be at issue. One can leave the Church, one can wound her, but one cannot suppress her. At issue here is the unity of the People of God, the unity of Catholics *in* the Church. Today this unity seems quite precarious. Without pretending to exhaust the subject, we should like to examine several data bearing particularly on this unity, and calling it into question.

1. *The place of personal option:*

By "personal option" I do not mean the matter of "personalism" of which Newman has given us so remarkably balanced and profound an analysis. Honoring this kind of "personalism" consists in recognizing that the Church is not only a wholly constituted and structured institution within whose framework we commit ourselves; the Church is also something *to be constituted* through the contribution of the personal gifts of each one and of all. One of the rather remarkable acts of the conciliar ecclesiology was the emphasis on charisms in our vision of things. These are the spiritual gifts of nature and of grace which correspond to the quality of our vocation and service. They are realities, says St. Paul, given for the common good and also for the harmony and congruity of the Church. Those who preside over the community should recognize and should foster the contribution of these charisms for the common work and growth of the Church, for the work of the ministry, for building up the body of Christ (Eph. 4, 12).

But we are speaking here of "personal option." This is not unrelated to the gifts and calls of the Spirit but it is also something else. It is the pursuit of a personal destiny through and, if need be, beyond or outside the institution such as it is given to us.

For a long time now the sociological unity of Catholics has been broken. In France this happened as a result of the need in the nineteenth Century to take a definite position with respect to the public law spawned by the Revolution: a public law which, for brevity's sake, we can call secularism, leaving to this word its ambiguity. Pius IX, taking secularism to be a rejection of any religious influence in society as such, condemned it. I have just finished re-reading the totality of the documents to which the Syllabus refers and I can say that Pius IX was correct in his analysis. But understanding this public law as a position of the non-confessionality of the State, some French Catholics accepted it, while others rejected it on the same basis. Leo XIII later decided in favor of the position of the former, while at the same time developing a very positive doctrine of the necessity of the social action of Catholicism. In a lavishly documented book dealing with the first thirty years of the *Catholic Association of French Youth,* Charles Molette cites the significant lines of Father Cormier (February 2, 1892) of whom Zigliara, in order to draw up the plan of what was to become the letter

Au Milieu Des Sollicitudes (February 16, 1892) had asked for an advance copy of the text. His idea was to prepare another *Syllabus* — one quite different from that of the Pope. The Pope's was rather *negative,* condemning the false pretensions of the worshipers of the Revolution. But his would be affirmative, teaching the means to do good in the conditions created by the Revolution.[1] It was to be a kind of encomium: there was no mistake that he warmly accepted all the social conditions and policies of the Republic. This debate has not totally outrun its course among French Catholics. It is no longer the object of overt discussion, but it does inspire in a latent fashion their all too real disunity, even today.

For the past quarter of a century, the positions taken from personal conviction in cultural, social or political matters frequently prescind from solidarities of confessional teaching or even dogmatic fundamentals. It thus happens that a Catholic often finds himself more in accord with a Protestant or even with an unbeliever than with another Catholic. Such associations do not take place solely on a one-to-one basis. They beget a communion of thought and of feeling, of common encounters in political action, a unanimity, or a community which eventually enters into competition with confessional community. The clearest example of this was provided in the interdenominational celebration of Pentecost in 1968 in Paris — a striking development of the thrust that today carries many Christians, especially the young, to express the harmony they have experienced on the plane of their Christian commitments in a common Eucharist. Clearly, the Eucharist is employed in this

37

case not from the normative data of its institution but in terms of the data of life and personal experiences. This poses a very serious problem, which involves even the signification of the sacrament: is it the act of the united and assembled Church, is it the act of persons expressing their personal communion in Christ? And where is the distinction between these two perspectives evident?

2. *Is unity given or is unity to be sought for and created?*

Under the signature J. P. and the title: "What is Unity?" *Temoignage Chretien* of November 14, 1968, published some lines in which an extremely grave problem was posed with a great lucidity. J. P. distinguished and set over against each other two conceptions of unity involving two conceptions of authority, or at least of its exercise. On the one hand "unity is conceived as the unconditional assent of the totality of believers to a global datum and to a uniform action." The role of authority is to prescribe the conditions of this assent and to keep the faithful within a constituted and given frame. It must be recognized that this action of unity exists among us Catholics and even that it is dominant. In the 19th Century, one hardly ever encountered any other kind of unity of action. We considered it to be valid and true, without, however, necessarily affirming that it exhausts the truth of the unity in question.

On the contrary, J. P. thinks that "the unity to be realized can refer only to a future (which is Jesus Christ) and that that implies confrontation and research." "In this perspective the (necessary) authority is not that which imposes adhesion to a content that it proposes, but that which the march, the consistent search of the group produces *beyond* and *through* the confrontations."

The difficulties that this proposition raises are immediately discernible. Is such an exercise of authority possible at the level of a body as vast and as diverse as the Catholic Church? Is it not, rather, the exclusive ideal of small groups whose members, in possession of a certain culture and of a personalized faith, agree at least on the idea of seeking and of going beyond? And if it were only a matter of this kind, namely, merely reference to the future in the confrontation of the search, and not of the already constituted and given, would it not seal the end of the unity of the Church?

The problem is quite real. To convince ourselves of this, it suffices to examine the conditions in which democratic man and technological man pose for themselves today the problem of authority. I am not endowing the expression "democratic man" with any political idea properly so-called: it designates simply a situation in which authority is viewed above all as the function that represents and harmonizes the concordant search of the participants: "That implies that authority appear as founded, not on the past or on acquired situations, but on the needs of the future and on the efficacy of having the common good in view."[2] Consequently, democratic man extends his hand to the man of the age of technology. The latter is habituated and even imbued with the conviction that today is better than yesterday, and that tomorrow will be better still. The upshot is that his interest, indeed the base of his life, is situated not behind him,

in the past, in the acquired and the traditional and
the wholly given, but forward, in the future, the
not-yet, in that which is to be sought. From this,
there derives a de-valuation of any form of authority
speaking in the name of rule or of tradition. Is it not
clear that these data constitute the same elements of
the problem posed by J. P.?

But, on the other hand, what is true remains
true. What God Himself instituted or pronounced
preserves not only its validity but also its imperative
and normative character. In the name of what is being
sought, we absolutely cannot disown what has been
given. Since 1937, we have met this false alternative
at the heart of the ecumenical problem: the unity *to
be received* and, in this sense, to be sought for *in
advance* should not make us neglect the already given
unity into which, having recognized it, we must
incorporate ourselves. But the problem is still broader. Since the same time we tried to formulate it in
terms of *alpha* and *omega,* categories which were later
developed in my book *Landmarks For a Theology of
the Laity* (1953, see pp. 98 f.1, 148 f; 211 f;
458-461). These categories signified that Christ is
already *given* (in himself, for us) and yet at the same
time he is yet *to be created* (in us and by us).
Between the two there is time, history, and the
development of our free action that fills history and
for as long as time is open to us. In this sense,
everything, even unity itself, is always achieved and
to be achieved, given and to be effectuated, "Gabe
and aufgabe," as the Germans say.

Accordingly, there is place for search and for
confrontation, on the condition that these do not

amount to a subtraction of what is already given. This introduces a rather inconvenient tension into the functions of authority, because each of the two conceptions that we have sketched have their truth. Unity too has, as it were, two sources. We are especially familiar with the already constituted unity in which the peoples of the Church must be kept together. It is an easier thing, it holds in store less adventures than "a unity to be created, based on confrontation." But it must also be said that it is a more vital thing, in the sense that a vital organ is necessary not only for growing but for keeping an individual in being and preserving its identity. This is one of the reasons why we rejected, not long ago, the procedure which dismissed progressivism and inte-gralism as if they were questionable values located exactly on the same plane (see the first edition of *True and False Reform in the Church*, 1950).

3. *A Critique of Unity obtained through con-frontation.*

I have always defended the need for the political non-commitment of the priest while at the same time recognizing the difficulty of sticking to it. The priest should be everybody's priest. He should try to conduct himself in such a way that no person would have an objectively valid reason not to be able to ask him to hear his or her confession. The Church is something more than a mere dimension or an animation of the world.

True, the Church has the mission of animating and enlivening the world and that, of course, means that Christians must engage themselves politically. They have often been overly timid, and frequently we

41

priests, who have so generally drawn on the bit and the bridle, are to blame for it. Instead of encouraging them, we have been rather constantly on the side of the powerful, of the established classes, that is to say, of those who today are called the forces of repression. On the other hand, while believing that we were not engaging in politics, we did participate in the work of different political programs: total severance and abstention are virtually impossible. But today, people take a wider view of political engagement; they argue that the Church necessarily has a relationship to what happens in history and in what is accomplished by her members. The people, they say, have their normal manner of exercising this responsibility, they can genuinely entertain serious doubts about something while the Church has a definite position, a manner peculiar to her alone. The stance of these people is that of political militancy. The manner of the Church is that of a prophetism and of a didacticism (an absolute witness and an unchanging teaching) bearing on man, his dignity, the justice which is his due, the love in which he must find his truth. This kind of position is not nothing; it is something; but it lacks pragmatism, it is absolutistic.

My own position on the political non-engagement of the priest is not personal to me. I recognized an excellent formula for it in the lines of Father E. Marcus, theologian of the Mission of France: "Priests should keep themselves on this side of commitments which would risk seriously compromising their pastoral relationship with believers and non-believers alike. Such would be the case, for example, if a priest

42

holds a position in an enterprise, a movement, a political party, a leadership of such a kind that one could legitimately accuse him of putting his spiritual autonomy (that which confers upon him his concrete responsibility for the Church) in the service of a cause to which a Christian is not necessarily obliged to adhere."[3]

This position, however, is rejected today by a great number of the faithful and many priests. The general context of their rejection is complex; the reasons for this are multiple and everything but negligible. Here are the principal ones: (a.) *The experience and the lessons of history:* Marxism (and even Marxists) we have known in France; and also Fascism (and Fascists). A certain a-politicism ill-advised us in the face of Nazism.[4] An ecclesiology too narrowly concerned to distinguish the Church from the world fosters the attitude for which Pius XII and the German bishops have been criticized, and for which a Bonhoeffer criticized the Lutheran Church of the years 1934 and thereafter: the latter feared "that the Lutheran Church will resist only on an intra-ecclesiastic line. When she is no longer attacked in her substance or in her order, will she not retreat, believing herself intact . . .?"[5] Yes, men of the Church court the danger of reacting to injustice only when it affects the institution-Church in her human aspects, not enough when injustice affects plain men and in them, man. (b.) A notable change has taken place in this regard in the past twenty years. We have a better understanding of *the political dimension of all human commitment, even religious.* (c.) *A true contact with militants of all types has contributed*

largely to the education of priests in this sense.
(d.) *Finally, these priests no longer want to be
clerics.* They want to be men fully and, quite often,
men completely *like others.* We have already seen
how a more evangelical comprehension of their
priesthood caused some to try to re-establish the
fundamentally prophetic nature of their priesthood:
that was and that remains an entirely valid step.
Today the tendency to "de-clergify" the priesthood,
which we have discussed elsewhere[6] brings the priest
closer to the layman. To be everybody's man, to hold
oneself "above the fray" appears as a mystification
that involves an a-politicism which they condemn as
illusory. To this corresponds a critique of the unity
obtained by non-commitment: an artificial and
empty unity, a unity of the lowest common denomi-
nator, a facade unity. For men are human in their
commitments. To unite them while forgetting this
truth is to unite men through what they are not, it is
to unite phantoms. On the other hand, if we take
human commitment in the struggles of the world
seriously, we are bound to wonder, and quite
radically, about the worth of this sham unity.

This is precisely what Joseph Robert has done
recently by posing the question of the possibility of a
common Eucharist between oppressed workers and
repressive employers: *"Can one eucharistically serve
the Lord and money?"*[7] To the question posed in
these terms the answer (theoretical!) can only be in
the negative. But it is also necessary to beware of
what we call Manicheeism which proposes alternatives
that are all white on one side, all black on the other.

Joseph Robert, without expressly taking up the

44

problem that he had posed, later presented an admirable meditation on the dimensions and the truth of the Eucharist, and compared current events to those which happened "on the eve of His Passion." So that our Eucharists may be truly in conformity with that of the Lord they must (he argues) realize these seven values: intimacy (warmth), fraternity, service, sharing, liberation (exigencies of justice), festiveness, prophecy.

In regard to inter-communion extolled by the impatient advocates of ecumenism, it has been said that unity of faith is necessary. True, but is that enough? Assuredly, it suffices for the validity of the sacrament. But does it suffice for making the celebration authentic? Some distinctions would seem to be called for here. If we consider a given individual person, his offering is deceitful from the moment that he harbors hate or injustice in his heart. *We* cannot judge it. It is possible that a personal *sin* of injustice does not correspond to an objective injustice. This obviously implies that one really has an intention of true justice and that one is prevented from making it objectively real either because of inculpable ignorance, or because of something outside the realm of possibility. But injustice can be patent and really imputable to us. In the ancient Church, the canons proscribed offerings coming from iniquitous operations.[8] St. Basil refused the offering of an unjust prefect.[9] Is it possible to apply such a rule today? How to do it while preserving the margin between subjective and objective guilt and the delays necessary for the chances of a conversion? How to honor the evangelical rule with its three conditions enunciated in Mt. 18, 15-17: face to face, among several brothers, before the whole community?

But unity is still threatened in a different way, even in its eucharistic expression and very summit. We fear that it may be gravely compromised if the principle of personal option gains the upper hand over the principle of institution in the public behavior of those who, in the community, functionally represent Christ as a head convoking, building and uniting His people, that is to say, in the behavior of priests. A Manifesto by some French priests, for example, demands that they be given the right "to take, according to circumstances, political, trade-union or other options and commitments." That forms part of a whole context. Concretely it is a matter of a Left-option, just as up to the beginning of this century it had largely been a Right-option. Some even say that it is a clericalism of the Left as before there had been a clericalism of the Right.[10] The latter caused us "to lose the working class." What will the former cause us to lose or to gain? This question must not be approached solely in terms of gains and losses, but in terms of husbanding resources and of evangelical re-interrogation, and in terms of a sound ecclesiology confirmed by the lessons of history and of experience. The Gospel was preached amid constant dramas of resistance and repression, but Jesus did not lose Himself in them. True, He was the universal savior whereas we represent Him at the head of a definite community, but the image cannot contradict its model. Did St. Paul assume any political commitments? Let us repeat: we do not advocate an abstention from commitment for man, for justice, for the promotion of every man and all men. Really to exercise such a commitment must certainly involve concrete options *for* certain causes and hence *against* certain others. That the priest can and should do. It is of such a nature that any Christian can join him and follow him in this (eventually, to be sure, and even very frequently precede him). It is not *that* which is contrary to unity — on condition that one works in a certain fraternal style.

This last point merits particular attention. Paul Ricoeur wrote not long ago: "My hope is that my Christian comrades who do not choose *the same thing* as myself, will identify themselves with me in the same *Christian manner* of choosing."[11] This "Christian manner" obviously involves determinations of content because the "manner" does not justify anything: there can be no "Christian manner" of being unjust or racist or traitorous in regard to the truth. "Christian manner" always requires that one be *for man*. But since the program is complex and since nobody among us is universally perfect, several solutions are possible: it is here that the manner of upholding and promoting them comes into play. What will be "the Christian manner" capable of saving unity in pluralism? First of all, we must have an obvious loyalty whose index is the disposition to love truth enough to change our opinion if one proves to us that ours is wrong. Secondly, we should have awareness of the limits of our choice: we cannot identify it purely and simply either with *the truth,* or with *the* position of the Church. As a consequence of this, mutual tolerance is so rare in France where every divergence threatens a return to the wars

of religion. Obviously, this tolerance does not signify
that all the options are equal to each other, as human
truth or as something in conformity to the Gospel.
Elsewhere I have cited Jean Guéhennos' remarks on
"the margin of fraternity." The phrase expresses a
golden rule.[12] It implies a real opening to exchange,
to dialogue. During the time of the student demonstrations in Paris, Paul Ricoeur had been in Nanterre.
He was one of those few people to whom everybody
could talk and who could talk to everybody. That
would be a rather good formula for what is truly
important for us to achieve.

I would like to add to these reflections a few
words which I know in advance are also quite
insufficient on the subject of those who are common-
ly called "integralists" or conservatives. I know that,
by so doing, I am imitating the gesture of the
simpleton who sat down upon an ant hill for a picnic.
Come what may! Love of Catholic unity impels me to
speak as well as the sorrow I feel, knowing that many
of them suffer from the belief that there exists
discrimination among the children of the Church.

The integralists can render a service to all of us
by making what is already constituted and given more
imperative in their lives. The minority at the first and
second Vatican Councils prevented what could have
been an excess on the part of the majority. If the
theological Commission of Vatican II furnished a
work that was finally so serious, it was due in part to
the active presence in its midst of some contestants.

There are conditions that conduce to constructive criticism. It should not be purely negative: it

should recognize the positive features of a certain program, ones pursued and contributed to by those whom it believes it is necessary to criticize. Nothing is so radically opposed to this necessary minimum than a radical mistrust inspired by the idea that a vast conspiracy exists to destroy the faith. It is hard to envision a fraternal peace comprising a legitimate pluralism if the integralists refuse, *de facto,* to admit that the difficult questions posed today are not reducible to a conspiratorial enterprise of subversion, that everything is not constituted and *given* and that there is reason to speak.

The integralists are not alone when they complain about the major weakness of an ideology: their opponents also succumb to it. It is a danger that lies in wait for all of us. By ideology here I understand the tendency to build a whole interpretation or a program starting from only a certain number of facts or passages of texts generally separated from their context. In this way, one can construct a heresy, expose it and pierce it with a sword. If it is a matter of persons and their writings, quite often we project an image in advance, like a cipher or a decoding device: we categorize, we label. Nothing good can come out of Nazareth. The integralists say that, but in fact, they too often are victims of this same thing. We must acknowledge this. But I, myself, have frequently been subjected to this treatment, and I am not alone. Conservatives also complain that they are kept in a kind of oblivion and silence: assuredly the great pulpits are not open to them today. I am poorly placed to offer them a good reply inasmuch as I am somewhat privileged in this regard. But I am sincerely disposed to extend my hand to any Christian brother, and first of all to any Catholic brother. But I ask of him that, in turn, he make an effort to approach positively, and not only in a negative and critical way, the difficult problems confronting all of us and to propose a constructive and valid contribution so that we may all patiently come up with a natural solution to our difficulties.

Four

A POPE RECITES HIS FAITH

Pope Paul VI concluded the Year of Faith with a profession of faith before an immense audience on June 30, 1968. This profession of faith won the immediate assent of millions of Catholics throughout the world. Nevertheless, it has also been disputed: we are referring to the remarks made by the pastor Lukas Vischer since the ecumenical Assembly at Upsala, and the critical presentation by Giancarlo Zizola in the *Informations Catholiques Internationales* of July 15, 1968.

There is a positive aspect to these critical reservations. Lukas Vischer deplored the fact that the Holy Father expressed a *Credo* several articles of which were denominational, not ecumenical. But the Pope cannot seriously be reproached for having formulated, even in a rigid fashion, the faith of the Church over which he presides. With respect to Giancarlo Zizola, his criticism shows that we have gone beyond the stage where an act of the most revered authority does not pass muster unless one appreciates its content, its tone, its impact on cultured minds. Saying this, of course, does not mean that we approve in equal measure all of Zizola's remarks. Is it, in fact, a matter of content? A Catholic accepts, obviously, a doctrinal statement of the Pope with that "submission of will and of mind" of which

51

the constitution *Lumen Gentium* speaks (No. 25).
Whoever says "submission of mind" says there must
at least be an effort to understand the meaning of
another. Now the meaning of the *Credo* of Paul VI, as
regards its content, is clear. The text is woven from
formulas drawn, at times, word for word, from
declarations of the ecclesial teaching authority, principally conciliar, from the Council of Nicaea and
other Councils up to Vatican II. By proceeding thus,
the Holy Father took an option whose meaning is
manifest: his Faith is, without addition or subtraction, that which the Church has formulated, deriving
from the apostolic deposit and its development in
history. It is an affirmation of continuity, of identity,
and in papal terms of apostolicity.

I said that the Pope took an option: an option is
nearly always fatal insofar as it grants a privilege to
one value while leaving the others in the shadow. The
option taken by the Holy Father is more retro-
spective than prospective. It entailed a formulation of
the Faith in terms of the past which we absolutely do
not disown, but which men of today do not always
understand without an effort which they hardly are
eager to make. Was it possible to express the same
content in more kerygmatic terms — terms better
adapted to the needs of the men of our times? And
was it also possible to put into the *Credo* certain
values cited in the conciliar decree on ecumenism
(No. 11)? We would be inclined to say yes. But
perhaps the Pope would have lost the significance of
his evoking the whole past of the Faith as still and
always present in the Faith of the Church today.

There is the text. There is also the gesture. There

52

is that which Paul VI expresses in and through his daily life and administration. Perhaps the Pope expresses himself more in his gestures than in his texts. This is most certainly the case in the sphere of ecumenism. Let us, therefore, try to understand the gesture of June 30 as such.

Consider the situation: the Holy Father presides over the Catholic Church in one of the most difficult moments of her history. She has known many other such moments, but never perhaps was everything called into question as it is today. Mixed with admirable resources (what century has had more evangelical resources?) and with very legitimate investigations, with authentic new elaborations, perhaps too many remarks might have contributed to shattering positions and beliefs considered as certain until now. We will gladly agree that several of these positions can be subjected to revision or to the search for a better formulation. But the mass of questions that have been raised, the imprudence and the radicalism of many of them are such that we cannot help but share the disquiet which the Holy Father has expressed more than once, his urgent admonitions accompanied (we should also note) by the declaration of his firmest will not to arrest or discourage any valid investigation.

What was the Holy Father's intention in this recitation of his faith? He did not wish to promulgate a syllabus, nor to give a sermon but only to set an example by placing himself at the head of the Catholic faithful, not as an authority above them, but as one of them, the first among them: "Here is my faith." By confirming his brethren, not by expressions of authority, but by the testimony and the communication of his fervor, by acting not through pressure but through inspiration.

This is a very evangelical and apostolic manner of exercising the responsibility of authority. John XXIII, who taught the world more through his manner of being than through the texts of his teaching office, loved to present himself as the good shepherd who walks in front of his flock, and all follow him.[1] How many times did St. Paul, who knew perfectly well how to claim his authority, prefer instead — he says so himself — to appeal to his spiritual gifts, to his example, to the fruits of his apostolate? The ministers whom the sacramental ordination and the work of the Church have placed at the head of Christian communities do not act on them only through the exercise of their function: in this very exercise, they act very powerfully through the example of their faith and of their prayer. The priest is a public man even in his personal life. Paul VI, amidst the still too worldly pomp in the din and tumult of great public demonstrations, appears most expressively as a man of prayer. We were witness to it in Rome and, thanks to television, in Jerusalem, in Bombay, in Bogota. In the Mass celebrated at the Holy Sepulchre in January 1964, in front of the tumultous throng, where a blackout could have spoiled everything, the intensity of the presence of the Holy Father in prayer had saved everything. The example of John XXIII showed that this wholly evangelical and spiritual way of building up the Body of Christ is singularly effective. May he who, after Pope John, today represents Peter in the midst of

men and at the head of the Apostolic body, lead us
into a unanimous act of faith and prayer!

Five

AUTHORITY, INITIATIVE & CO-RESPONSIBILITY

There seems to be agreement on the deepest cause of what one could rightly call the crisis in the Church today: it has developed from the impact of the general crisis in civilization. We are justifiably disturbed over so many acts of militancy, over-initiatives of a quasi-anarchic character. It would not serve any great purpose, however, to re-affirm the legitimacy of authority if we make no effort to understand the reasons which call it into question, if not perhaps in itself, at least in the forms of its exercise as handed down till now. This is why we propose here, while holding to the most general level of discussion, to recall the foundations and the nature of authority, after which we shall offer an interpretation of the reasons that call it into question today. Such a procedure will allow us to pinpoint many of the demands touching on its proper exercise. Finally, we shall try to conclude our study on a positive note and in a linear perspective.

1. *Nature and Justification of Authority.*

The word authority "displeases" today: it is a disagreeable word for many of our contemporaries and Christians themselves are somewhat allergic to it. Its employment (exousia) was very limited in the New Testament and was applied primarily to the ministers of the Church.[1] St. Paul affirmed indeed that he had power, authority. But it is remarkable that he prefers to appeal to his spiritual gifts, to his example, to what the Spirit has wrought in him,[2] rather than to his exousia. What term shall we employ, if we wish to avoid "authority"? "Governance" is not any better. "Power" says the same thing. "Pastoral hierarchy" is the most proper, above all in consideration of pastoral needs, which is the main biblical consideration, but "hierarchy" is a creation of Denys, the pseudo-areopagite, who lived between the 5th and the 6th centuries. So many words and usages are confusing so let us preserve "authority" at least in the present chapter.

What is power, what is authority?

Power is defined as "the possibility that a man has of making his idea and his will prevail over others in a particular social system." Authority would be the right (and the contingent corresponding duty) which a man has to have his idea and his will prevail, etc. In short, between power and authority there is a transition from fact to law, and it is indeed the shading that one finds between *potestas* and *auctoritas,* for example, in the famous text of Gelasius I, in 494: "Duo Quippe Sunt . . . ."[3] In short, *Authority is the right that a person has to determine something in the life of other persons.* We understand that our contemporaries, smitten with individual freedom and with the autonomy of the personal subject, are restive before any authority and before the very idea of authority. But that presumes modern individualism which has largely ended up with a mentality of a foundling, without father or mother. Modern man not only wishes to view himself as autonomous: the creator of his own future; he does not recognize himself as a child of the past, dependent on paternal roots.

It is not in vain that the notions of authority and of authorship exist. The right to determine something in the life of another is exercised in the situation in which, in order to be this or that, indeed before all else, simply in order to be, one thing is dependent on another. There exists only one absolute authority, that of God the Creator. After that, the first authority created is that of the parents, the co-creators. What can one determine in the life of another more than parents: his nationality, his sex, his heredity, his social and cultural chances and most fundamental of all, his very existence which in the circumstance, is definitive in its spiritual and physiological characteristics and consecrated to eternity? This is what parents do. Accordingly, one understands the profundity of the Fourth Commandment and the bond by virtue of which the religious attitude toward God is pre-formed in that which one has toward one's parents, one's country. These are precisely the realities for which language reserves the word "piety" — which involves the affectionate and respectful recognition of this dependence on a reality from which we have the determination of our very being.

This is why the respect for parents is the preparation and the preformation, as it were, of the religious attitude. Those who undermine this respect, the books or films which without let-up ridicule adults in order to glorify the non-conformism of young people, attack the natural bases of religion,

which it is absolutely vain to contrast with the Faith.
Let us recall the commentary of *Erat Subditus Illis* by
Charles Peguy: Jesus "brought this Fourth Commandment to its full realization, to its whole supernatural
potency. For the obedience, the submission of Jesus
to His foster father and mother, so perfect in itself
and of a teaching so eternal, were still only a
temporal image, a carnal representation of the eternal
filial obedience of Jesus to His Father who is in
heaven . . . ."[4]

How is this philosophy of authority applied in
the Church? In society, public authority is such
because it assures the common good, the *Utilitas
Publica,* by harmonizing, promoting and organizing
the public order (static aspect) and the expanding life
of society (dynamic aspect).[5]

But civil society does not create its members;
the Church, in a certain fashion, creates hers, she has
a maternity. There exists in the Church, of divine
institution at least as regards her principle (if not as
regards her form, save perhaps the function of Peter),
a ministry ordained sacramentally, a ministry of the
faith and of the sacraments of the faith, of communitarian unity and of service or a diaconate of charity.
If we wanted to express ourselves in terms of the
common good, we could say that on the Christian
plane the common good is the salvation (that is to say
the true and successful order in God and in the
creation) obtained for humanity in Jesus Christ. The
pastoral authority derives from the fact that it
procures participation in this common good, and this
not only *de facto* but reckoning from its principal
institution by Jesus Christ. Hence, this pastoral

authority is linked to a sacrament, that is to say, to an *Act of God.*

Obviously, things are such because, as the Dogmatic Constitution *Lumen gentium,* No. 9, states: "It has pleased God, however, to make men Holy and save them not merely as individuals without any mutual bonds, but by making them into a single people, a people which acknowledges Him in truth and serves Him in holiness." Compare *Ad Gentes,* Nos. 2 and 7. "There is no salvific revelation made privately to each one nor any salvation accomplished for each one in isolation: there exists a single public revelation, a single common and public salvation of which one becomes beneficiary in the People of God to which the Lord has given structure."

Let us conclude, therefore, that there exists, in the Church, a hierarchic pastoral ministry having authority, and a faithful flock of brethren and, therefore, that there also exists a faithful-pastor relation — "secundum, sub et supra," according to superiority and subordination.

It is not enough, however, to pose in the Church a hierarchical principle to which the reality of the institution corresponds. This is what has been done, and all too exclusively, in the frame and in the climate of an ecclesiology reduced to public law as that stands out from the history of ecclesiological doctrines (we ourselves have written one). Fortunately practice often escaped this exclusivism of theory, but it was hampered by it. The Council has returned to a deeper tradition and, without denying the principles of institution and of the hierarchy, it reopened the possibility of an ecclesiology of the

People of God and of an ontology of grace on a sacramental basis. The most crucial chapter of *Lumen Gentium* is that of the People of God with its theology (resumed in Ch. IV) of the spiritual priesthood and the place that it makes for charisms. Thus another principle again finds its place, the *personal principle,* which we shall discuss later: it opens into the communitarian (and not only societal) reality. The order of succession of Chapters II and III of *Lumen Gentium* signifies that the first reality is that of Christian persons animated by the Holy Spirit and that the structures of authority, of society and of institution are in the service of the life of persons.

True, there exists a danger in the affirmation of the personal principle — a danger rather profusely illustrated by Protestant individualism from which contemporary Protestantism is trying precisely to heal itself. The modern spirit tends in this direction. It is not true that persons are reducible to individuality. There is not in us only an individual without human reference or roots, and therefore without dependency. We are not only individual persons, but also and indeed first of all, human nature (this is the metaphysical basis of the fact of original sin), members of a society, children of parents and disciples of teachers, sharers of a common good of life qualified by a culture and a history.

Christian life being at issue, here, the latter can be described essentially as a communion deriving from the participation in the same principle of existence: the charity of Jesus Christ, that is to say, in more concrete terms, Jesus-Love. There cannot be an explicit Christianity without community, nor without entry into the historical chain of mission, of preaching and of sacraments that bind us again to the positive and historical fact of the redemptive Incarnation: Christianity is social and instituted: *social,* it is the supernatural and even divine consummation of the natural unity of men.[6] *Instituted,* and even divinely instituted, it is the historical and positive form of the Covenant, constitutive of the People of God.[7]

2. *Present Difficulties.*

It seems to us that three large headings should be opened here. This first will spread over three lengthy paragraphs and, because of this, will be of a more extensive character.

A. *A certain man, dependent on a certain historical moment and climate.* Moment and climate today seem to us to engender a man who qualifies himself as personalist, democratic and conditioned by technological progress.

1. *Personalist:* Personalism, before being modern and coloring itself with individualism, even subjectivism, is a Christian value whose influence is already disclosable in the confrontation between Christian thought and ancient paganism.[8] The latter was dominated by a very cosmological view of a stable, hierarchized world — and let us not ignore that in its image and in its frame Christian society was constituted. Ancient and medieval Catholicism often took up these themes, sometimes even by borrowing many views formally from pagan authors. It had situated the personal usage of our freedom in an objectively given order which issued norms to it:[9] for man was a microcosm, an epitome of the world. It is

true that the idea of a transcendent order and of social models has, to a good measure, acted as a brake on movements of liberation, and prevented Christian reflection from developing a theology of broad social change. The fact remains, however, that Christianity in depth has been an affirmation of the person, of his free determination, of his free initiative in this determination of the grace of God and of the freedom that procures this grace. What we have called the personal principal cannot be sundered from the principle of institution or of hierarchy.

This involves the recognition, one remarkably granted by the Council,[10] of the role of charisms in the building of the Church. Everything does not proceed from above, through the paths of the institution.[11] We must recognize the place of personal gifts and of initiatives in which the freedom of the Holy Spirit acts. It would be wrong to see in man and the Christian only a being determined by factors that transcend him and dominate him. For there exists this personal principle of consciousness and of initiative which constitutes an immense richness. The person, reduced to his individuality, is poor and feeble: he needs to fulfill himself in an exchange and in communion with other persons. Experience superabundantly confirms what present-day philosophy, one of whose themes is choice, tells us. This is an experience that we underwent at the Council. In a short space of time, there was a blossoming and a maturation of the ecclesial consciousness on very difficult points, thanks to this communication of minds that the great fraternal assembly, in which the Lord was present, permitted. This is only a major case of what can and should be effected in the Church: it is significant from the point of view of the exercise of authority. This shows in fact that there exists a deeper way of determining our behaviors than the way of a decision handed down from above by authority, namely the way of a maturation of personal consciousness in the bosom of a fraternal community. In this regard, the Council represents a remarkable union of the personal-communitarian principle and of the principle of institution.

If we may be allowed to prolong these considerations by the evocation of a recent event, we should like to state that, in a recent intercelebration of Pentecost in Paris between Protestants and Catholics, it was the personal-communitarian principle alone that spoke, and which took no account of the principle of institution or sought to harmonize itself with it. There was a gesture expressing a personal Christian attitude and even a real community of persons, but not the gesture of *The Church* as such, structured through the apostolic institution. We cannot conceal from ourselves that this is the danger today, when the law and the institution appear so easily as alienating factors; one wishes to be oneself and freely to sing one's own song. Whereas, in I-II St. Thomas presents the law as being (from without) with grace (from within) an auxiliary of true self-realization, through the coincidence of our will with the good.

The personal principle, authentically Christian, has assumed a new character in our time. With the advent of modern times, one passed from an objective, fixed and hierarchized world, in which a person saw himself situated in an order totally comprising all the created, to a world in which the subject affirms his own subjectivity and his free personal choice. The fixist-hierarchic view had been carried to its most extreme form by the defenders of theocracy and of hierarchy at the end of the 13th and in the beginning of the 14th centuries: a Boniface VIII and Giles of Rome, for example.[12] It was very precisely denounced, along with hierocracy, by William of Ockham (d. 1349) in the name of a philosophy of freedom and of the individual. In the name of the free will of God and of what He can do on account of His absolute power, Ockham rejects the (so-called) necessities and proprieties founded in an order of the nature of things; in the name of evangelical freedom and of an affirmation of the individual, he wishes maximally to limit what is imposed. On the religious plane, the modern revolution began from that moment. If Luther calls Ockham his beloved teacher, it is probably because he was the first, in the name of the individual person and of Christian freedom to overthrow or contest the whole hierocratic and papal order imposing itself as law.

Modern philosophy is probably little concerned with making a connection with its antecedents. Nevertheless it is, in the same line, a philosophy of subjectivity, of the autonomy of the free personal subject. It has ceased to be, and even to try to be, a comprehensive interpretation of the world in order to become a reflection on man, on the conditions of existence and of knowledge. The roots of the difficulties which we run into today are philosophical. Young people, consciously or not, participate in a philosophical current for which the point of departure is not an external objective given, but oneself. It is a question of interpreting oneself to oneself in contact with the world, with others, and even with the Gospel and the Church or the different institutions that exist in the latter. Clearly, the subordinate-superior relation is affected by it. Tradition, obedience appear as a domination of the object, of the cut and dried, and therefore as a bullying, an alienation harmful to the free realization of the subject. The series of personages that Albert Camus studies under the title of *The Rebel* illustrates to the extreme the attitudes that we are trying to define. We recall that the reason advanced in this work by Camus in order to reject Faith was the will to assume responsibility for his own life by himself; religion assertedly robs us of the loftiest duty incumbent upon us, that of being a man who himself assumes the risk of his freedom. The concern, we could say the obsession with sincerity peculiar to our time conduces to a view of institution that reckons only from personal convictions or projects. Doubtlessly the substitution, so frequent, of the word "project" for those of vocation and of mission is a sign of this. The horror of any pharisaism, the aversion for any legalism, do not end up only with the liquidation of a certain conventional Catholicism; they risk turning into disregard of any objective order which might impose itself on the subject and to which the latter should adapt himself. We have excerpted this significant sentence from a long letter in which a student (a very serious Christian) tells us about the events of the Pentecostal celebration in which he had been actively

involved: "One witnessed with enthusiasm an extraordinary phenomenon of communication — people
began to talk to each other and then, above all,
people became capable of listening and inquiring and
nobody had a ready-made answer." Let us likewise
consider the possibilities for success in the open-
ended conversation. The subjects have a need to
express themselves without *a priori* imposing any
barrier on them. It is that, perhaps, which is the
ground of "contestation."

2. *A Democratic Man.* This modern
attitude has, as it were, institutionalized itself in the
structure and the climate of our democratic societies.
In an article of July 5, 1824, when the "Restoration"
was in full swing, Chateaubriand, an observer of the
transition from one world to another, wrote: "The
monarchy effortlessly re-established itself in France
because it has the force of the whole of our history,
because the crown is worn by a whole family that all
but saw the nation born, which formed and civilized
her, which gave her all our liberties, which made her
immortal. But time has reduced the reality of this
monarchy. The age of fiction is over in politics; we
can no longer have a government of adoration, of cult
and of mystery; each one knows his rights; nothing is
possible outside the limits of reason. Today everything is weighed, everything is judged, even royal
favor itself, that last illusion of absolute mon-
archies." [13]

The sacerdotal hierarchy will always preserve a
certain sacred aura, but it can no longer exercise its
authority as it did in the former climate of cult and
of mystery, inasmuch as the whole society is estab-

lished on different bases. Father J. Dubarle describes the change which, on account of this fact, has occurred in the manner of viewing authority and compared it to the former situation of "theocratic mystery" as follows: "Whence this new democratic ideal of a society built through the rational cooperation of wills placed in objective situations and uniting their human possibilities? The 'head' is the one in whose being and initiatives the concert (rational? — in principle, yes, rational) of wills recognizes itself. In dialectical terms, the democratic individual obeys his own will in the person of his 'head' in whom he discovers, promoted to be the representative of reason, the reflection of his own will. For the model of divine authority notifying the human being of his commandments as they are at the level of the Old Testament, contemporary spirituality substitutes, more or less directly, the 'neo-testamentary' model of Jesus Christ, Head of those who recognize themselves in Him. . ."[14]

It is therefore inevitable that the man of today, living in a democratic climate and amid democratic structures, wishes for a less Jupiter-like (to borrow a term of J. Folliet) exercise of authority. This all the more so inasmuch as the faithful are demanding to be treated as adults, not as minors. They want to assume their own responsibilities. They ask leave to speak and to be listened to in spheres in which they have the feeling of competence and the duty of being active or co-active in determinations that concern them. For they, too, are the Church, and not the simple material for a "Church" which would consist of clerics. But the latter are not exactly always the last in wanting to de-clericalize the conception and the governance of the life of the Church. In this regard, some even propose that we share with them some elements of democracy which, perhaps, are questionable.[15]

Whatever the hypothesis, we must preserve the joy of the experience that exists today of pooling, of exchanges, of dialogue, of joint research, bringing together people belonging to different categories and who for years had been close to each other without truly engaging in an exchange among themselves. Today we are invited to live more really real relationships of fraternal communion.

3. *A Man Conditioned by Techno-logical Progress.* The man of today has witnessed achievements to which, without posing to himself questions of critical valuations (which would involve the application of criteria), he attaches a value of progress. Children surpass their parents in so many spheres! Young people have the feeling that the truth lies ahead, not behind. They give their faith to the future, to what has not yet been. They are less prone to take as teachers those who transmit acquired certitudes than those who shake them and open up the paths of the future. The men of tradition are barely listened to. Authority, which represents the acquired and the fixed, is contested on principle.

Younger persons tend to believe themselves beings without a past, to ignore their roots, to deny any worth to what has preceded. It would be easy to find in recent happenings an illustration of the Oedipus complex: the murder of the father, whose place the son would take.[16] Or, something which

70

certainly has connections with that, a search for brotherhood without fatherhood, a community without other dependence save that of the horizontal bonds among the members.

The three values, personalist, democratic and tension toward a future of progress through cooperation, the last two in particular, have contributed to the transformation of the ideal that one fashions for himself of a unity or of an authority which, at bottom, corresponds to it: for the essential function of authority is to assure unity in the form of the common good. But this unity itself can be viewed in two ways: either as constituted and given, in which case it is a matter of maintaining it or of leading the members of the group to it, or as something to seek for and procure in advance, in which case authority is principally a function of animation and of the harmonization of efforts. One does not expect from it — and one is close to not tolerating from it — the intimation of a decided form of existence or of action. "In these perspectives, the (necessary) authority is not that which imposes adherence to a content that it lays down but that which provokes beyond and through confrontations the march, the consistent search of the group."[17]

For a long time this way of considering things has found its application in the sphere of ecumenism: we remarked earlier how some people risk not honoring the unity already given since the time of Christ and the apostles in the expectation of, in the search for, a not yet given unity. Another wholly natural application lies in the freedom of inquiry which the personal principle encourages and the actual existence of personal gifts which suggest values irreducible to those already held. The applications to the liturgy have been sketched here or there, more often in practice and *via facti* rather than in a theoretical way. This is the claim of creativity which, in our opinion, translates an authentic need, even in the sphere of the liturgy.

It is necessary to recognize that the effort called forth by the situation that we have just analyzed is far from being incumbent only on the bearers of authority. The superior — subordinate relation is bilateral. Its truth according to a new style depends on the faithful and on priests as well as on the bishop and other authorities. But, in regard particularly to the third feature that we have pointed out, we must lay stress on the necessity of new elaborations in the theological domain. We should, in fact, take note of a certain insufficiency of classical expositions in the sphere of ethics: this without denying or failing to appreciate the worth of these very elaborations. They are in fact precise, but offer only an inventory of known, confirmed and fixed duties. In them we find no trace whatsoever of what there is a felt need for today: an ethics of engagement in advance, in the not yet come-to-pass. After having arrived at the threshold, the word fails us. Men address themselves to other teachers. Everywhere today we hear the demand for a "theology of Revolution." The matter calls for examination. But we are overly habituated to standing fast in the assured precincts of the recognized, of the fixed, of that which does not prepare us for a surprise.

B. *The Church as a Community of Brothers.* The truth of the faithful — pastor relation must be sought in the frame and in the light of the ecclesiology re-established by Vatican II after six centuries of juridicism and four centuries increasingly dominated by the unconditioned affirmation of authority. The Council, as has rightly been asserted by Father Schillebeeckx, has effected a vertical re-centering on Christ and a horizontal de-centering toward the totality of the People of God.[18] Cardinal Suenens has clearly shown how the Council, at all levels, has substituted for the solitary exercise of authority a spirit of co-responsibility and structures of co-responsibility: at the level of the Holy See (collegiality, synod of bishops), at the level of priests (presbyteral board), at the level of religious both male and female, and at the level of laymen (pastoral board, organisms of Catholic Action, etc.).[19]

The most crucial prophetic step of the Council in matters of ecclesiology through the chapter *De Populo Dei* of *Lumen gentium* which it was decided to place before Chapter III *de Hierarchia,* was its recognition of the primacy of the attribute of *Christian,* or of the ontology of grace inaugurated at Baptism in regard to any juridical structure with the relation that it involves between members *"Secundum, sub et supra."* What is most fundamental in the Church is the Christian existence of faith, hope and charity, of charisms or natural and supernatural gifts ordained to building the Body of Christ. It follows that the Church is a fraternal communion all of whose members are living and active.[20]

The functional relation of inequality is nevertheless not destroyed. It must clearly be recognized in
this regard that there exists today a certain way of
making use of the idea of the People of God and
therefore of conceiving of the latter in ways which
are not entirely correct. Often today, some faithful
demand freedom of decision or embark on an
undertaking, declaring: we are the People of God, as
if the expression had the political meaning of
"people" set over against the rulers, as if it designated
a simple sum or undifferentiated mass, not a structured community. Such was the erroneous use, in the
history of ecclesiology, of the classic definition of the
Church as *"Congregatio Fidelium"* made by Ockham,
by the nominalists, and by the Protestant reformers.
Lacking to it is a mysterial and sacramental dimension that this definition involved in its classic usage in
the 12th and 13th centuries. Since its origins, the
Christian fraternity has been a hierarchically structured community, and this on a sacramental basis at
the same time as on a juridical basis.[21] All in it do
not have the same vocation, the same function, the
same responsibility. But all are concerned, all are
co-responsible. When I was preparing *Landmarks for
A Theology of The Laity,* I conducted a rather deep
investigation through history and tradition. And I
found in them the constant co-existence of two
principles: a principle of hierarchical structure, a
principle of communitarian exercise of life and of
authority itself. The latter goes very far back in time:
I gave examples, cited testimonies, and it was to
express this principle that, in 1953, I restored the
word "collegiality" to currency. I studied it in one of

its boldest formulations, often invoked in the 13th century: *"Quod omnes tangit ab omnibus tractari et approbari debet."* (Title of an article published in the *Revue Historique de Droit Franc et etr.,* 1958, pp. 210-259).

The same conclusions would be arrived at reckoning from a study of the paternity of the apostolic ministry in St. Paul. Assuredly, the Apostle says that he is the father of Christians when he has evangelized (1 Cor. 4, 15; Gal. 4, 19), but he would not fix the latter in a position of sons. If St. Paul and St. John employ this word, it is as a quality of tenderness, not of situation, because spiritual paternity does not beget sons, it begets brothers because it leads to communion with the same good and the same life, in dependence on the same true Father (cf Matt. 23, 9; Eph. 3, 15). It is much more profound than the program expressed in the Arab proverb: "When thy son has grown up, make him thy brother;" this is an exigency of Christian ontology.

There exists a hierarchic fact, but this hierarchic fact situates itself entirely in the fraternal union of the baptized. Here one could comment on the text of St. Paul: "And his gifts were that some should be apostles, some prophets, some evangelists, some pastors and teachers, for the building of saints (Christians), for the work of the ministry (diaconate), for building up the body of Christ" (Eph. 4, 11-12). There is a work of the diaconate which consists in building the Body of Christ: it is incumbent on all Christians. The role of functions or ministries is to organize Christians with this work in view. From this view of the hierarchic functions within the baptismal community derive the three following consequences that concern our subject:

1. The hierarchy, the Pope himself, is not above the community, but in it. This excludes, in our opinion, certain formulations of papal primacy or infallibility which would make of it the monarchic source of all power, of all doctrinal certitude for the Church. In this frame of the baptismal community, we can appreciate the correctness of this assertion of Father Laberthonniere: "The exercise of authority in general is only one of the forms of what we must do, each one for the other and all others for each one, in view of our common destiny."[22] Laberthonniere is wrong to believe (p. 40, footnote 3) that the way in which St. Thomas situates this fact himself in the larger frame of the cosmos would destroy the personalist aspect of the relation: in truth, St. Thomas' view is fundamentally that.[23] We are a body full of thinking members (Pascal), a community of persons in which each one of whom, at one and the same time, has his own personal fate, and in which all have the same destiny. In regard to the former and the latter, the relations are solidarities existing among us: in short our brothers, our neighbor, have an influence on us; it is in relation to them that I must situate myself vis-a-vis God and in the line of salvation. But among these brothers and this neighbor those who, on the basis of divine ordination, have the right to determine something in my life, are for me situant in a more radical, more decisive fashion. The relation that unites us for the accomplishment of our common destiny and of my personal fate and which is a relation *"secundum, sub et supra,"* is assuredly

"one of the forms of what we must do each one for the other and the others for each one," but it is a decisive form of it.

Moreover, here we must exactly define two points concerning this influence on me of a brother who, through his function and his ordination, has become my superior. To begin with, insofar as this influence is due to his function as such, it is limited to the competence of this function. It is not because X is bishop that he can determine something in electronics. But a hierarchic minister does not act only in carrying out the acts or in exercising the privileges of his function. The priest is not just the consecrator of the host, he draws a community into prayer; the way in which he celebrates, the way in which he speaks of God and of the spiritual life, likewise *act,* even have a concrete efficaciousness that can be very great. This possibility is not peculiar to the priest, but it intervenes in the exercise of the actions that are proper to him.

2. He is a baptized person, qualified by the essential conditions of Christian existence, who is eventually constituted in a position of authority. In that case, not only does he remain a Christian and must, as such, pray, convert himself to the Gospel, love, etc., but his attribute of Christian qualifies his function of authority itself. This is what we have tried to show in studying the hierarchy as service.[24]

Authority in the Church is a *Christian* authority: it represents a qualification for presiding, directing, organizing, which affects a Christian whose law of existence is gift through love and service. Thus service is something different here than a nuance added from the outside and dependent on personal spirituality: it qualifies authority intrinsically, insofar as it is a Christian authority.

3. In these conditions, finally, we must lay stress on this point, which is decisive in the heading of authority and of obedience: the superior and the subordinate pursue and serve the same good. The relation that unites them should not be conceived only in two terms: the authority does not by itself place itself in a position of superiority; constituted in this position, it seeks and serves the same good, the same truth as the one who is subordinated to it. Thus, without denying its obligations, obedience assumes an aspect of cooperation, of co-responsibility and, therefore, to some degree, of dialogue that does not signify that the superior is only a brother with whom one discusses and decides *ex aequo*. Rather, this signifies that he is actually a brother and that each adapts jointly to the good that both the one and the other seek.

It is not a matter of imposing on subordinates only that which they determine themselves, like parents who obey their children in everything. Authority must be subject to the realities and to the ideals to which it can eventually lead along with the very persons whom it must command. St. Benedict rightly says that, sometimes, God reveals His will through the most humble (Regula, c. 3). If we go beyond the point of view of the single structure *"secundum sub et supra"* and of obedience as a simple means of the order to be maintained, of a responsibility to be honored, then authority and

78

obedience are exercised in dialogue without thereby
reducing themselves to the equality of dialogue.[25]

C. *The Inviolable Rights of our Intelligence.* One last fact should be considered very
carefully among those which make obedience more
difficult today and which call for a new effort in the
exercise of authority. Let us try to analyze it by
proceeding from the most peripheral to the most
essential.

The contemporary experience of revolutions
such as the Resistance, the wars in Algiers or
Vietnam, the movements of Camillo Torres and of
"Che" Guevara, indeed even the experience in the
Church of pioneers who were censored or bullied at
first and then honored and followed, and of other
similar experiences, have had the effect on younger
people of making them keenly feel the distance, if
not the conflict between the formal legitimacy of an
authority and the truth of an act that bears with it
the moral justification of this act.[26]

It is very important to see that present-day
militancy is generally inseparable from its object or
from its content. Doubtless there exists a small
number of individuals who fight just for the sake of
fighting and who attack simply in order to demolish.
Generally we are in the presence of individuals
smitten with the thirst for authenticity and sincerity
who battle whatever, rightly or wrongly, they do not
understand. That does not mean it necessarily be-
hooves us to follow them, but we must first of all
listen to them and accept their request for an
explanation in order to re-establish or to re-discover a

transparence and an authenticity of the meaning.

In matters of liturgy, for example, or of religious observance, younger people do not tolerate the imposition on them of a way of doing things whose meaning would not be justified in terms of their consciousness and their sincerity, but be imposed as a law, through the authority that has conveyed it or through tradition. At most, the only authority on the basis of which a behavior-pattern could be imposed would be through perception by the subject of its meaning or utility to the exclusion of the role of the authority seeking to impose it. The latter would be merely the executant, necessary for the proper running of things which the free consciousnesses belonging to a given group independently desire or accept. Moreover, this manner of viewing things, in which the formal reason of authority and of obedience is obviously lost, was not born yesterday.[27]

The danger is very serious. It cannot, however, justify the misunderstanding of an essential anthropological element: obedience is addressed to the voluntary decision of a man who is equally intelligent. It can ask us to accede to a decision that goes beyond the evidence available to us; it can bid us to revise our evidence. But it cannot compel us to contradict absolutely the proven evidence of our consciousness. Here two critical remarks force themselves on us in regard to the state of ideas in Catholicism.

       1. The objective and transcendent norm of action is mediated by the consciousness in a complete conjuncture that comprises the objective norm but without a detailed design given in advance.

At stake here is the whole originality of moral action. Remarkably enough, St. Thomas understood this but he himself is not always understood and followed. Contemporary reflections could lead us to a better comprehension of this important article of anthropology and of ethics.

2. We have allowed formal legitimacy, either that of a decision or that of a power (for example, Marshall Petain) to prevail too much over the real content or over the reality of a spiritual good to be sought for. This is discernible as much in the domain of the theology of the sacraments or in the theory of apostolicity where (in the theology of the books, if not in practice) only the formal, ritual and juridical conditions of the "apostolic succession" have been considered.[28] The law of the Sabbath has often got the upper hand over man. Doubtless we have not believed enough in man. In the 19th century, after the jolt of the French Revolution, the Church lived with the obsession to constantly reaffirm authority and everything that could be construed as personal evaluation or preference was eliminated as "rationalism" or "free inquiry." Historians pursuing this line of thought could examine the expressed or implicit anthropology of the official ecclesiastical documents, of the hagiographical criteria, of the works of spirituality on which the clergy nourished itself and theologians could examine their conclusions in the light of a biblical anthropology. What is the source of the fact that the clergy had had for so long and so spontaneously a kind of psychological connivance with the authoritarian or military forms of human conduct? What accounted for the

81

hold of casuistry and of legalism over morality? Have we not excessively maintained man in tutelage under the Law?

These remarks entail certain conclusions which, though they are no doubt difficult to honor, are nevertheless important, touching on the exercise of authority and that of obedience. It would injure the nature of both to reduce them to the communication of reasons on the one hand, and to the evidence of their good grounds on the other. But it would also injure their truth not to insist on the intellectual grounds which the authority should adduce and the subordinate be free to accept in terms of reason. It has been said: "The attribute peculiar to authority is that it does not have to give reasons." This is a curious statement, for by it one gives a formal-limit condition to authority, and one which obviously does not exhaust the question.

3. *Conclusion.* We shall consider briefly three points: 1) the exercise of co-responsibility; 2) militancy; 3) the exercise of the pastoral teaching authority.

1) *The exercise of co-responsibility.* Co-responsibility inheres in the logic of fraternal communion. The Council set it in motion at all levels: cf. the book by Cardinal Suenens and the form given to the updating of the religious life (all the members of a community are to be consulted and given an opportunity to express themselves). It seems that the Council has perceived the mutation of the world and that the steps it took have not been without influence on events. This very fact is signi-

ficant: there was lucid perception because there was fraternal assembly. May we not expect an increment of perception of the movements and demands of the world from a broader practice of pooling our energies?

First condition: information. If one expects great effort from the faithful, the issue involved must be explained to them; and starting from the what, the why and the wherefore. We can take as an example what is being done by the communist mayors in many communes around Paris, where they have chalked up considerable achievements in the way of improving facilities and equipment at the communal level. That presupposes a method of financing such expenditures, hence the imposition of additional taxes. And they obtain them because they explain the reasons for them and show that additional taxes will make such achievements possible.

We need information to flow in two directions. Clerics should be better informed by laymen on the life, ideas and plans of the faithful. Not in order to lose themselves in sociology and journalism, but for the purpose of working better at their own level and delivering valid words. This is a fact: laymen still complain of being too little listened to by priests and of the slight inclination priests exhibit to engage in dialogue. They say that the formation of priests is not conducive to a more responsive attitude in this regard.

Obviously, it is necessary to create participatory structures. That does not signify an increase in bureaucracy, but it does signify meetings, boards, an effort to "be in the swim," with a certain share in administration or in decision-making. We have already seen the example of the synods of Santiago (Chile), of Rouen, of Holland, of Ceylon, of presbyteral or pastoral boards.

A particular point: the part to be played by the faithful in the designation of ministers. We do not see the possibility of coming, or returning, to their direct election, nor to the ordination of persons designated more or less despite them by the bishop or by the people.[29] Let there be no romanticism! But in the course of his formation the candidate should go through a probationary stage before the diaconate or as a deacon. In this way he inserts himself in a community of Christians who will intervene in a very effective way to form him. The community will effect the maturation of a minister who, in a certain way, will emanate from it: before the ordination, in a visit to the bishop, and on the day of ordination publicly, some faithful will come to bear witness in regard to the one whom they have known and assisted in becoming a minister of the Gospel.

2) *Militancy.* Applied to the Church the word hurts, above all because it is associated with excesses, abuses, and the danger of ushering in chaos. It is imposed on us. Therefore we should proceed with an effort of discernment: such a process, moreover, could succeed only in dialogue.

The present-day demand for the right to militancy is inseparable from the motivation or from the *content* of this militancy. It would be futile to exclude any right to any act without examining the reasons. Young people claim the right to contest *that whose meaning they no longer understand* or whatever appears to them to be associated with social structures that they reject and that seem to alienate them from themselves. Accordingly, their militancy is connected with the crisis of civilization at large.

We see no possible solution save in the acceptance of our problems today and tomorrow, while preserving a keen awareness of the values that are to be held onto always — and all this in a climate of active patience that presupposes an actual mutual trust. By active patience, we understand the behavior of one who does not jump instantly, or rashly, to conclusions but knows that delays are necessary. The person who practices this patience does not confuse it with a dilatory attitude, but he actually works with the combatants in the give and take of dialogue in order to prepare a solution.

There are things that militancy cannot be in the Church: it cannot do the following: 1) Destroy charity or act in such a way as to surround its acts with circumstances of a kind that would wound the heart of charity; or destroy the unity of Catholics even to the point where they would no longer be able to break the eucharistic bread together. The question is not so simple. Neither can one, in the name of this unity, emasculate any questionings and searchings, sterilize any efficacious and concrete engagement of people, any commitments they might make. 2) Question the hierarchic pastoral structure such as it comes from the institution of the Lord. 3) Deny or even question in a hasty and unreflected or irresponsible fashion articles of doctrine for which one should be quite ready to give his life. 4) To classify once and for all and without being careful of the margin of fraternity all those who think differently from us in the category of wicked persons; to make a cross over them as over the damned who are without hope. 5) We cannot allow expressions of militancy in the liturgical celebration and particularly in the sermon. That would create an intolerable climate of irritation and provocation. On the other hand, questions can be discussed here or there in some nearby premises or even, as in the United States, immediately *after* the sermon.

On the other hand, we accept militancy if it signifies that everybody can actually express himself and be heard. For example, the conditions that obtained at Lille, on June 17, 1968, in the Church of Saint Peter-Saint Paul, where there was a meeting for exchange and discussion, strike us as sound. This is a new form of this "free speech in the Church" which Catholics were demanding before the Council. But it is a truly new form because it is more collective, more spontaneous, more alive, more related to topics of the hour (with the dangers this involves of introducing passion and of not respecting the true proportion of things).

For our part, we believe the following consideration to be illuminating: when a question is very complex, it can *legitimately* give rise to several approaches and therefore to several judgments, hence no one can pretend to exhaust the totality of the givens. Accordingly the possibility of another option and other conclusions than one's own must be admitted. True, not all are equal in regard to realities and even in regard to the gospel. There are some that are more intelligent, whose views are more in consonance with the gospel. But the person who thinks differently from us also has reasons that he views as valid.

3) *The Exercise of the Pastoral Teaching Authority.* If the need to contest is insepar-able from the malaise, the causes of which are expressed in the content of the contestation, those who have a teaching function in the Church should try to respond to the questions. Whence the urgency of what Msgr. Elchinger calls a pastoral activity of the intelligence. At bottom, it is the task of theology. Today the latter has changed its style. From a consistent elaboration (at best, systematized) of a normative *given,* which kept it in a cultural climate of the Church, theology has moved on to be a reflection on the faith, on its possibility, its meaning and its essential content in a cultural situation determined by the movement of the world: the latter determines the work to be done. In these conditions, the crisis of civilization has a direct impact on the problems relative to faith and on the theological task. The ground of the problems posed today is philosophical or philosophico-critical. We have emerged from a naive approach to revealed affirmations; man is the first given, in relation to whom these affirmations must be interpreted: man-to-the-world, man-in-situation, man in events. Inevitably, in comparison to the former state of things (to which a man of my age belongs and of which he is painfully aware), one has the feeling of entering into a condition of insecurity. Moreover, in a way that we can consider contestable, younger people pitilessly denounce any "security-giving" situation or effort. They situate and establish

themselves in insecurity, and seem to thrive on it.

If this analysis is correct, the teaching Church must obviously promote philosophical and theological research and in some manner be educated by this research. But this research itself is not the monopoly of a few licensed theologians. The decisive reflection can be born in the person of a teacher of science, in a meeting of students, in the course of a review of the activities of some group, etc. The whole People of God with its charisms is the locus in which the reflection on the faith is to be elaborated. That does not simplify the task. But ultimately it is necessary that men and women dedicated to this work come together and elaborate the proper elements of a solution. Today one finds sociologists, workers, everybody, but one hardly finds theologians. Let us transcend the word "contemplation" which could be ambiguous. Nevertheless, we must arrange the time and the conditions of calm, religious attention and for meditation on the Word of God. Without that the presbyteral or episcopal priesthood will never be able to deliver a word that nourishes the faith.

The teaching authority has gladly been "defining," above all since Pius IX, and that was accompanied by an over-estimation of this very office, by an absurd abuse of the category of what is "infallible." Today we are brought back to more evangelical authenticity: the *witness* of the Word of God must dominate over any pretension to define. In the present crisis of authority and of obedience, we cannot be sure that the best parry consists in the multiplication of affirmations of authority as the

Holy Father has done. To bear witness to Jesus Christ, the Incontestable One, and to His gospel would be the most efficacious way through which authority, while forgetting itself, would re-discover itself.

The conditions of the exercise of the pastoral teaching authority are still more complicated for another reason. From the spirit of the Council of Trent there has emerged a certain type of bishop who was intensely committed to be the shepherd of his people. But the people were Christian or disposed to be such, and as a result society did not go beyond the limits of Christianity and of a culture congenial with the Church. Today, the world is wholly different and it has, precisely in this difference, a density and an urgency never felt hitherto: it is the world that imposes its problems, its own categories. From Vatican II there has emerged a Church and a number of pastors whose plan and resources aim at service of the world in its specifically worldly problems. The pastors know themselves to be pastors not only of a Christian people but, in a certain fashion, of all men — even of those who do not have the faith. The pastoral teaching authority tends to assume the task of enlightening the faithful and even all "men of good will" in terms of their life-problems in the world and in events. This is an aspect of a prophetic priesthood, and not simply a cultic one.

That commits the corresponding theological effort, even at the level of the teaching authority, to being much more *inductive*. This is the epistemological problem before which the Council found itself with *Gaudium et Spes*. Quite naturally, during and after the Council, five secretariats, which are organs of dialogue, information, inductive knowledge, were created in Rome: non-Catholic Christians, non-Christian religions, non-believers, Justice and Peace, laity. This is one of the conditions of the new exercise of the pastoral teaching authority.

There is another condition that likewise concerns the epistemology of the pastoral teaching authority. Taking the word in a non-strictly dogmatic sense, pastors should first of all bring to the world the affirmation of the Word of God, while especially developing what it contains of light for man today. But they will often have to go beyond that and it is here that a new form of the teaching authority to which the German bishops allude in their recent collective Letter will take on importance. The pastoral teaching authority should publish directive-documents which would not pretend to give a conclusive and definitive, magistral teaching, but propose first stages of reflection, an improvable teaching offered for the consideration of the faithful without excluding criticism or/and disputation.

Six

BISHOP ROBINSON: IS HIS WORK "THEOLOGICAL PORNOGRAPHY?"

Robinson's[1] intention is clearly stated. He himself expresses it by quoting this conclusion from a review of *Honest to God:* "The book is fundamentally not an essay in unorthodox theology, but a venture in evangelism." We would say, perhaps more accurately, that it is catechetical. Robinson wants the man of today, the man of the post-Christian era, to hold firmly to Christ even if he cannot accept *as realities* certain miraculous happenings: the star and the angels of Christmas, St. Michael's struggle with Satan (cf. Jude 9; *Rev.* 12, 7-12), the multiplication of the loaves, the angels in white seated on the stone of the sepulchre, the virginal conception of Jesus.

Robinson's way of dealing with these matters is simple. He states that the stories or statements were made in an obviously untenable imagery and he says: this story, this statement are not necessarily to be taken as representing what transpired. Their authors were simply expressing in an imagery acceptable to their times and in a language geared to their own keen awareness of the non-commonplace, the extraordinary and transcendental character of what they witnessed. For example, those who knew Jesus and who welcomed His message in their hearts felt that He was "rooted in a security that couldn't be

explained simply in terms of a human family back-
ground." They translated this awareness into the
affirmation of a miraculous, divine conception. Likewise, "the marvels of the night of Christmas are only
a way of expressing the significance of the event for
us. In that baby, and in the man who grew from him
is to be found the clue to the meaning of all life." For
the men of biblical times, that was translated into
these representations and corresponding images: God,
who is up there, has come down to us. He is present.
According to the ideas of the times, it was necessary
to have angels and celestial choirs. And so forth.

Is there any reality to anything? There is one
thing to which Robinson holds. He works out his
various criticisms in order to preserve the chances of
maintaining the reality of Jesus Christ for today and
tomorrow — the reality of Jesus as revealing the
ultimate reality and the deep meaning of the universe
and of our own existence as "a new kind of living, a
new kind of loving, quite out of the world," and thus
"a truth, a way, and a life that can give coherence and
meaning to everything in our experience."

All this is a reality irreducible to our world, and
therefore divine — a love perfectly realized in Jesus
Christ, a "Man for Others." The miraculous is only a
translation of the event in the imagery of an epoch:
it's peripheral, and it suffices to wrest from it only its
meaning.

We could walk side by side with Robinson or
follow a parallel route to his on the level of intention.
Many have preceded him for a long time even though
he gives the impression of breaking new theological
ground. A simple example. In the first book of his

career as catechist-journalist, Robinson strove to criticize the expressions *up there, out there,* as applied to God in order to describe His transcendance. He criticized the spatial imagery that makes us speak of Jesus "ascended to heaven" and "seated at the right hand of the Father." Was this a matter of a spatial transfer and, if so, how long did the journey take and as far as where? Would God have a right hand, would He be seated? A long time ago, Thomas Aquinas had written: "that which is described as having a local position in the world of bodies must be interpreted in terms of relation in the world of spirits." We speak of sitting at the right hand of the Father: it is an image that simply translates the fact of having received communication of the royal power of God, like a minister whom the king allows to sit at his right hand to mark that he has given him full power. It would be impossible sufficiently to stress the ambiguity of religious imagery: representation of the miracles of Exodus in *The Ten Commandments,* illustration of the Gospels, hell or purgatory, and the apparent quasi-totality of hagiographic images. Spontaneously, and in a first impulse, one naively believes that something transpired *as* it is represented to us. This is obviously not true, but should the first suspicion, the first rational objection risk shaking the faith at the same time as it questions the imagery? The Jewish tradition offers a very remarkable example of the problem: it is ten times more exuberant than the Christian tradition in evolving stories or in statements about miracles, whereas it is quite strict in not allowing figuration and images. Its stories, its miraculous statements aim to communicate meaning, and there is no attempt to determine what this meaning is. That remains enveloped in a certain haziness, but Christian tradition allows representation. It imposes strict limits upon it if it concerns God Himself: One must hold fast to the images given in the Bible. Further, it is expedient sometimes to explain them — and one may do so respectfully and in depth: for example, the dove in regard to which Robinson expresses himself rather flippantly. As for the rest, it is exuberance with its dangers but also with its admirable richness. In some cases it may be necessary to explain them in order to avoid the compromises of an excessive naivete. Thomas Aquinas says that in treating of divine things the crudest images are the best because they do not beguile us with the temptation to believe that reality is what they suggest. This point can be an argument in favor of the non-figurative. But one should not exclude the figurative. All that is necessary is to criticize it intelligently. When Matthias Grunewald represents the resurrected Christ by using the most extraordinary resources of his palette, it is clear that he translates his faith as he can conceive it and does not claim to achieve a documentary accuracy.

But we might ask ourselves: what would photography have yielded to us in the "blessed night" from holy Saturday to Easter? Would it have captured some special image, and which one? What would it have added to the question of the empty tomb? It is not a question of pictures, but of *how* things transpired? And what about those physical apparitions of the resurrected Jesus? The Gospels show Him present, touchable and even supping with His disciples. But at the same time, they speak (as St. Paul speaks) of apparitions: and the disciples, at first did not recognize the Lord. It is He, but not as before.

Here we find ourselves before the essential problem of the dangers of suspiciously critical reflection on the affirmations of sacred History. There is a question of expressing in the terms and images of our work, of the world of our earthly experience (we have no other), the happenings and/or the realities of another world of which most of us have no experience. Those who have, and whom we call the mystics, have expressly told us that they could not describe it, or could do so only by employing a language, hyperbolic or dialectic, denying what they affirm at the very moment in which they say it — as we see, for example, with the Blessed Angela de Foligno, who saw in her words on God so many blasphemies, so much did they betray what she wanted to utter; or in Denys, who spoke of "the very luminous obscurity of a silence full of profound teachings."[2]

We speak, for example, of the days or years of purgatory. It is obviously inaccurate since it concerns a world not regulated by the diurnal movement of the earth around itself or by its annual movement around the sun. No doubt it would be better to abandon such modes of speaking. But how are we to explain duration? That of the other world is wholly different from ours, but how can we talk about it if not in our categories? What is the life of Christ resurrected? We can speak of it only in the terms and in the images of our experience, of the inadequate character of which, however, we become aware only after some minutes of reflection. Our expressions would amount to a lie were we to claim formally that the reality was, or is, exactly *such* as we express in the terms of our world. Hence, we affirm something whose objective reality we are incapable of translating save in a fashion that we must recognize as inadequate. There is no way of doing otherwise. Naive faith, that which suffices for the poorly educated, has no need to pose these questions to itself. But reflected faith, the faith tested in the fire of rational criticism, must. Let us add that we do not want to suggest any depreciative nuance by use of the term "naive faith."

But how do matters stand with Robinson who wants, in short, to place reflected faith in the service of naive faith? We believe that he would concede the correctness of the remarks we have made above. He might even say that they could be incorporated in his own plans and projects. He would underline only the confession of nescience we ourselves have made in regard to supernatural reality, and emphasize that he not only wants to ignore it but that he does not even care to interest himself in it and would leave it in the sphere of the unknown, indeed the indeterminate. As such, he professes a deliberate agnosticism.

It is here, no doubt, that we part company with him. Indeed, even in the matter of expressing our agreement with him, let us recall that we spoke not of following exactly the same path but a parallel path. It's one thing to criticize our expressions and our representations in regard to a reality the objectivity of which we unqualifiedly maintain: this is the procedure that we pursue. But it is a horse of another color, while theoretically treating with caution a nescience of what this reality is objectively, to reduce concretely the content of what it signifies *for us,* or more accurately to what I realize of its signification for me. Robinson does not deny that there is more, he professes simply that he has neither the capacity nor the wish to unravel it. Practically, however, he effects not only a reduction of expressions adorned with images as applied to a reality that is not positively representable, but a reduction of the reality to what it signifies for me or even, let us repeat it, to what I realize of its signification for me, and for my life as a man.

Inasmuch as the "reduction" bears not only on the expression but on the reality, there is a great danger of dissolving the supernatural element which has been thrust into the history of the world and into the mind of earthly man. That is a legitimate fear; for example, when we read in regard to Good Friday "that the truth about Christ's death is the truth about their lives," and in regard to the Return of the Lord, that to believe in the *Parousia* "stands for the conviction that — however long it takes — Christ must come into everything. There's no part of life from which he can or will be left out."[3] Finally, the advent of Christ is totally reduced to his coming to us in our neighbor and in events: "Everywhere, at any moment, Christ comes in."

Is there not in such utterances a danger of the reduction of the other world to this world, — and not just ways of speaking about the other world to those of speaking about this world here? Is there not a denial of the other world? Robinson does not explicitly do this, but he reduces everything to Jesus

Christ and to his special conception of Him. Have we not got the right to demand of those who speak to us of the realities affirmed by the Christian Revelation that they at least preserve them?

To fail to do this is not enough and that is why Robinson's catechetics cannot be adopted. His intention is praiseworthy; the shock that he administers can be salutary. We consider unjust — even though we must take it with a dash of humor — Karl Barth's utterance in regard to it: "It's theological pornography." But we believe that a Catholic cannot read his facile, all too facile books except by adopting a critical stance toward its method. What is finally at stake is this: does the history of salvation, of which Jesus Christ is the center and crown, simply add love as the deep meaning of our life (it does this, assuredly!) or is it not also the irruption into our world of another world?

Robinson does not deny that it does, but the way in which he thematizes his questions begets a danger of misunderstanding the whole matter. His success bears within itself the risk of betraying his very intentions and thus is doomed to failure.

Seven

THE CHURCH: MY MATERNAL HEARTH

The experiences of life have helped me to understand the Church more deeply and to appreciate her for what she is. It has befallen me, more than once, to be as if cut off from my human roots. There was captivity during the war, imprisonment in a fortress and later in a camp: this was the experience of exile in a climate of suspicion. In this connection I cannot help thinking about my time in a hospital which, despite the quality of the care, is a little like being in jail. During these various periods, I realized what a profound place is held in our lives by an affective bond with a familiar setting which, by its real name, is called the hearth. This is something quite different from a mere sentimental attachment. It's something beyond formulation in clear ideas, something involving a vital incorporation of our deepest self, something pre-reflective and yet charged with truth — something that began before us, is beyond us, yet surrounds us and supports us in all we do. We live in a "setting" like a fish in the water, but the setting also penetrates us, its woof is entangled in the web of our lives.

We human beings also experience a vital need not to be alone. Aristotle said that a solitary is more or less than a man: *aut bestia, aut deus,* a brute or a god, but not a man. For ordinary humans, nothing is

more destructive of their humanity than total solitude: not the moment of solitude that can, on the
contrary, foster plenitude and fulfillment, but the
moment of rooting-up, isolation, abandonment. And
if such solitude is carried to the point of dereliction,
we would be in the vestibule of death.

For these reasons Jesus promised us that he
would not leave us orphans, without a hearth.
Orphans we Christians will never be: there is the
Father, who is in heaven. But Jesus has thought of
our earthly solitude too. In his last testament, the
profound echoes of which fill chapters 13 to 17 of St.
John, he took precautions for the time of His bodily
absence, by promising us the Spirit and by giving us
an apostolate. The circumstances that accompanied
his death, and again St. John is the solemn witness,
are equally significant. Jesus gave up His last breath,
emisit spiritum, on John, the disciple, and Mary, the
Mother, who represented the Church at the foot of
the cross. Then the soldier pierced the side of Jesus
asleep in death, and from it flowed water and blood.
The Church Fathers and the writers of the Middle
Ages have unanimously seen in this a symbol of the
sacraments through which the Church is built. The
water symbolizes the Spirit, and the blood the
baptism and the Eucharist. Here is what Jesus leaves
us: the Spirit and the Bride. Just as Eve had been
formed from the side of the sleeping Adam, so was
the Church, the new Eve, formed from the side of the
crucified Christ. In the two cases, the symbols
signified the unity of two persons called to form a
single flesh, a single body, in the love of spouses
destined for the fecundity of maternity.

100

The religious and, if you please, the theological reflection of the Ancients is at once very simple and very profound. It defines itself in the basic terms of life and maternity: just as Mary who, fecund through the Holy Spirit, gave Jesus to the world, so did the Church of Pentecost beget Christians for the apostolate through space and centuries of time. "And of Zion it shall be said that she is a Mother, for all were born in her" (Ps. 87, 5). The Church is, as Hugo Rahner magnificently says, "the Mary of the history of the world." Such a reflection is completed by reference to the mystery of the Redemption: issued from the cross, the Church is, by birth and by nature, sacerdotal, consecrated to offering and to being offered: she fulfills herself in the eucharistic act.

Jesus has left us, but in order to be still with us during the time of his physical absence he has given us His Spirit and His Bride, the Paraclete and the Church. Together they prepare the Kingdom and together they pronounce that happy word on which *Revelation* ends: "Come!" (22, 17). We will no longer be alone, we will no longer be without a hearth. The Spirit is our Comforter, our Defender, our Protector. Who ceaselessly assists man in the trials of the world, who enables him to be a disciple of the Gospel. We must often call upon this Spirit of Jesus, trust in Him, attribute to Him the good that can pass through "our empty hands." Just as the Spirit is a principle of outward unity, His presence is so inward that His testimony is almost indistinguishable from the movements of our own mind. He is intimate and personal: not "private," but given, as St. Paul says, in our hearts. It is He who brings together the "only one

101

with The Only One, me and my Creator," according to Newman's formula. And it is He who is "the spiritual hearth" for us brothers and sisters in the Church: the foundation and principle of Christian life.

Assuredly, there is a lot of narrowmindedness and immaturity, many botched works in the Church. We see in too many spheres how unprepared the Church is to offer answers to the true questions posed by men. But all that, as heavy a burden as it may be for us to bear, is of no importance when it is balanced against what I can find and actually do find in the Church. The Church has been, and is, the hearth of my soul; the mother of my spiritual being. She offers me the possibility of living with the saints: and when did she ever prevent me from leading a Christian life? In the midst of doubt and of tempests, the Church is always worthy of the grace that dwells in her and in the host of witnesses of which the Epistle to the Hebrews speaks, thanks to her memory and to her consciousness of self which are her living tradition and which operate in such a way that the Church never succumbs to doubt. Yes, we may deplore certain Roman reactions: the tone and harshness which irritate but whose perspicacity we cannot fail to recognize. Listen to the witness of Father Lacordaire whose eloquence was not diminished even by the precision of Roman formulas and condemnations directed against him personally: "O Rome, after so many centuries, I have found thee upright, ever virgin, ever mother, ever mistress. Seated amidst the storms of Europe, there was never in thee any self-doubt, any lassitude.[1]"

Is this too high-sounding, is it too idealized a picture? Perhaps, but in these expressions there is much truth.

I cannot find words sufficient to thank the Church for having made me live, for having raised me, in the strongest sense of the term, to a sense of order and beauty. She put order in my life, in my mind. True: there exists a certain taste for order, or rather, a taste for a certain order which is quite capable of wiping out the hunger and the thirst for justice. But my Church has repudiated such a betrayal of the gospel. It is also true that Catholicism has encumbered itself with many baubles and surrounded itself with many distressing esthetic mediocrities. But they are being disposed of rather well. There then remains the incomparable beauty of the liturgy in all its forms, in all its formulas, in its partition of time along the thread of days and seasons. Have we not many times relived the experience of Augustine who recalled in his *Confessions* his attendance at the Church of Milan: "How did I weep in the hearing of Thy hymns and canticles, touched to the quick by the voices of Thy sweet-attuned Church, *suave sonantis ecclesiae tuae vocibus commotus acriter"* (IX, 6, 14). Estheticism? Such an utterance could lend itself to that charge, but it could also be perfectly authentic and proper, if it is true that man is a whole and that he inserts himself in a hearth through his sensibility and his heart as much as through his ideas.

My hearth, the Church, has been an assured and peaceable place for my faith and my prayer. And why not? Quite a few messages, which have their element of truth, speak today on behalf of disquietude: it seems that a man who exhibits no impatience, who is not tormented by problems, is a laggard or simple-minded, and that agitation and anxiety is the normal stance. It is true that a certain calm could be tantamount to insensibility, that a certain peace could be the sign that one has betrayed one's vocation, that one has furnished oneself with an alibi or gone off on a tangent. It is of the impious that the Psalm says: "They are not in trouble as other men are" (73, 5). There is a way of taking shelter that would be a form of fraud. But once we acknowledge this, we cannot approve the a priori bias that there is no rest for man, nor the mania to criticize everything which can be related to peaceful assurance within the frame of the Church. But the liturgy does not speak the language of disquietude to us: much more, rather, it speaks of the peace and the grace which it ceaselessly implores: "Ut ecclesia tua tranquilla devotione laetetur!" Our Churches formerly were, legally, places of refuge. Ought they not to realize this vocation in a new manner, accommodated to modern man — winded as he is by competition, crushed by the complexity of everything, enervated by the din, intoxicated by indiscreet, insidious and aggressive advertising? Ah! blessed be the peace of my hearth — the Church!

FOOTNOTES

Preface

[1] W. J. Hollenweger, in *Vers une Eglise pour les autres,* Geneva, 1966, p. 154

Chapter 2

[1] See P. Colin, *Le prêtre, un homme reconnu, adapté, situé,* in *Prêtres d'aujourd'hui,* January and February 1966, pp. 12-22 and 82-91; by the same author. *Le prêtre, un homme "mis à part"* mais non "séparé", in *Vatican II. Les prêtres. Formation, ministère et vie (Unam sanctam,* 68), pp. 261-274. See also the Chronicle by M. Peuchmaurd in *Parole et mission,* no. 33, April. 1966.

[2] In the expression of their own position the priests of the Mission of France, on the whole, confirmed this diagnosis: "In a world of *Christianity* priests really participated in the social life merely by virtue of the fact of their function in the Church. It is no longer the same today. To many people priests appear as the standing personnel of an alien and useless institution wholly unrelated to the problems of man." (Note published at the beginning of December 1968).

[3] B. Gardey, *Pour quoi je vis.* Paris, Cerf, 1968, p. 61.

[4] Categories in which, for example, P. Schoonenberg expresses himself in *Le Prêtre et le monde sécularisé",* special number of the Information Bulletin of the Institute for Priestly Mutual Aid in Europe (Maastricht), February 1968, pp. 59 ff.

[5] This has not been properly elucidated in recent studies. Thus H. Denis, *Approches théologiques du sacerdoce ministériel,* in *Lumière et Vie,* no. 76-77 (1966), pp. 151-152, 154; F. Vandenbroucke, *Le sacerdoce selon Vatican II,* in *Les Questions liturgiques et paroissiales* 1966, p. 108 (with reference to B. Botte and to P. Grelot. This functional value does not

abolish the ontological permanence of the character of the Order, but it could well relativize its exercise. History, up to the 12th century, presents too many facts in this sense for us not to acknowledge a certain social (ecclesial) and canonical conditioning of the application of the principle: "Thou art a priest forever."

[6] See the *Treatise on the apostolic tradition* which employs the expression *cheirotonia,* imposition of hands, for the bishop, the presbyter and the deacon, chaps. 2, 8 and 9, but only that of *katastasis,* institution by nomination, for the widow, the lector and the sub-deacon, chaps. 11, 12 and 14. Hippolytus himself underlines the difference.

[7] Following a sacerdotal session held at the Seminary of the Mission of France, at Limoges, I had, in October December 1964, written a work entitled *Mission Sacerdoce-Laïcat* (Mission Priesthood-Laity). It was at the printers when the question of worker-priests was sorrily settled, with some repercussions in the French Dominican provinces (February 1954). Desirous to avoid anything that might magnify the crisis and, perhaps, even harm the cause I wanted to serve, I withdrew the manuscript from the printers. In it I had defined the mission: to be-with, as Church, with a view to Jesus Christ. An echo of this work is found in the article *Jésus Christ en France,* which appeared in *La Vie intellectuelle* of February 1954.

[8] See the beginning of the books of Hosea, Amos, Micah Zephaniah, Isaiah, Haggai, Zechariah.

[9] W. Bulst, *Israel als signum elevatum in nationes,* in *Zeitsch. f. kathol. Theol.* 74 (1972) 167-204.

[10] We are not expounding these questions here for their own sakes! There would be so many other things to say! Let us just note still another point that more closely concerns our subject. It is impossible to treat "Sacrament (sign and means) of

salvation" in a static way, as a reality existing for itself in order for a power to exist in the world that escapes the world and even prides itself in being superior to it. The Sign-Church is dynamic; it *is* mission: just as Christ is the Envoy of the Father: this is said without misunderstanding the doxollogical function of the Church and of Christ alike. Vatican II perceived the being and the life of the priest in the light of his ministry, in subordination and in succession to the mission of the apostles.

[11] K. Rahner, *L'apostolat des laïcs,* in *Nouvelle Revue théologique* 78 (January 1956) 3-32: pp. 20-22. We have noted elsewhere the insufficiency of these considerations for defining Catholic Action properly so-called: *Sacerdoce et Laïcat,* Paris, Cerf, 1962, pp. 329-356.

[12] L. M. Dewailly, *Envoyés du Père. Mission et Apostolicité.* Paris, Orante, 1960; J. Dournes, *Le Père m'a envoyé. Réflexions à partir d'une situation missionnaire.* Paris, Cerf, 1965.

[13] Thus in R. Shaull, *The Christian World Mission in a technical Era,* in *The Ecumenical Review* 17 (1965) 205-218, referring to Th. Van Leeuwen, *Christianity in World History.* London, 1964. These authors are Protestants. This may be involved, *one tells me,* in the case of Hubertus Halbfas, whose teaching mandate at the Pedagogical School of Reutlingen has been withdrawn by the German bishops.

[14] In the following manner. Today one speaks, at times, of "post-ecumenism". By this term one often understands that which is also called "secular ecumenism": The Christian service of the world, pursued together, in the more or less explicit perspective of the Lordship of Christ. It can be a very effectual path of approach toward unity. But, at times, it would appear that this alone suffices and that the unity personally obtained in the *secular* service of the world is the substance of Christian unity and the very goal of ecumenism. This time, we are no longer in agreement.

Chapter 3

[1] Ch. Molette, *L'Association catholique de la Jeunesse française 1886-1907.* Paris, 1968, p. 13.

[2] J. M. Le Blond in *Etudes* July-August 1966, p. 104.

[3] E. Marcus, *Les prêtres après Vatican II,* in *Prêtres et Pasteurs (Eglises en dialogues, 6). Mame, 1968, pp. 147-148.*

[4] In the sense that, though doctrinally opposed in a non-ambiguous fashion, to racism and Nazism the heads of the Church all too often remained on this side of what they were duty-bound to do because of the lack of a political consciousness. This emerges clearly from J. Duquesne, *Les catholiques français sous l'occupation.* Paris, 1966 and Guenter Lewy, *The Catholic Church and Nazi Germany,* McGraw-Hill, New York, 1964.

[5] A. Dumas, in *Foi et Vie,* May-June 1966, p. 97. For the German bishops G. Lewy, op. cit. passim. Pius XII concerned himself with the possibility of improving religious life for priests interned in concentration camps and also for Christians of Jewish origin. Cf. J. Nobecourt, "Le Vicaire" *et l'histoire,* Paris, Seuil, 1964, p. 184. It would be interesting to study the theme that we are touching upon here historically. A reference note for an eventual file: Innocent III reproving the Venetians, *Ep.* IX, 139 (PL 215, 957).

[6] Shall we de-clergify the priesthood? See chapter 2.

[7] *La Lettre,* no. 120-121: August-September 1968, pp. 1-3.

[8] See *Constitutions apostoliques* II, 8, I and IV, 5-9 (Funk I, pp. 196-197 and 225 ff; Council of Elvira (300-303 or 313-314), c. 28 (PL 84, 305); *Statuta Ecclesiae antiqua,* c. 69, pub., Munier Paris, 1960, p. 91 (= Gennade de Marseille in 470-485; councils of Auxerre of 585, c. 17 and 9th of Toledo, 675, c. 4 (Mansi 9, 913 and 11, 27).

[9] See Gregory Nazianzen, *Orat.* 43, c. 52 (PG 36, 564). Cf. St. Augustine, *Sermo* 355, 3-5 (PL 39, 1571-1572).

[10] Thus Pierre Debray, *A bas la calotte rouge!* Paris, *Table Ronde,* 1968. But is not the author, in his turn, placing himself on the plane of politics: simply on that of an opposite politics?

[11] *Le Semeur,* May-June 1950, p. 433. This notion of a "Christian manner" of acting merits elaboration. J. Maritain, referring no doubt to his idea of "acting *as* a Christian," for his part, writes: "Wherever there are human relationships, the Gospel, if we live it, introduces of itself its testimony, through the manner in which we act." *(The Peasant of the Garonne)* Trsl. by Michael Cuddihy and Elizabeth Hughes, New York, 1968 pp. 211-212.

[12] Here it is: Let our ideas be tidy; let us expound them in all their rigor. This is the condition of loyalty. Let us serve them with all our energies. It is the employment of our courage. But, just as we leave a margin on any sheet of paper on which we write for improvements, corrections, for everything that we have not found, for the truth for which we still only hope, let us leave the margin of fraternity around our ideas." *(Figaro,* January 6, 1951).

Chapter 4

[1] Homily pronounced on the day of his coronation, November 4, 1958 (Cf. *Documentation catholique* 1958, col. 1475) with citation of Jn 10, 16 and 21, which Leo XIII had already cited in the encyclical *Satis cognitum,* 1896. Here it is not only a devotional theme. The different studies by T. I. Jiminez-Urresti on the injection of primacy in collegiality shows that the theme has a rigorous or ecclesiological meaning.

Chapter 5

[1] With respect to our subject there are hardly any precise words save 1 Cor 9, 6 and 2 Cor 10, 8. For other terms expressing authority see our study cited in the following footnote (p. 80).

[2] This feature is extremely noticeable in the Apostolic writings. Paul knew how to argue over his authority as Apostle for the purpose of giving orders (1 Cor 7, 10, 17, but he also knew how to give counsel as a spiritual man by appealing to his experience, to his grace (Ibid. Cor 7, 10, 17). Rather than to the authority he possessed: cf. 2 Cor 10, 7-8; 11, 23 ff; 12, 1 ff; 1 Thess 2, 7-12; Phil 8-9, he preferred to appeal to the gifts that he had received, to what he was *ex spiritu* (for many, moreover, he was precisely that by reason, and in view, of his attribute as Apostle. Would we not find something analogous in Jesus Christ Himself who, by constitution and authority, is the perfect High Priest but whom the epistle to the Hebrews shows us as still in the process of becoming such through His sufferings and His personal feelings? In ancient Christianity cf. Barnabas 1, 8; IV, 6, 9: although having a doctoral title and a great erudition the author, among Christians, wishes only to one among them, and to speak to them only in the name of his love. Cf. our article, *La hiérarchie comme service selon le Nouveau Testament et les documents de la Tradition,* in *L'épiscopat et l'Eglise universelle,* Paris, 1962, pp. 67-100.

[3] Denz.-Schönmetzer, no. 347.

[4] *Un nouveau théologien Monsieur Laudet,* 111: Gallimard, 1946, p. 34.

[5] We are not claiming here that political society would be merely an extension of familial society, nor that it would not have an originality proper to it.

[6] A theme remarkably developed by Fr. Sertillanges in *L'Eglise* (2 vol. Gabalda, 1916; 6th ed. 1931): a work that deserves being remembered. It is an idea deeply rooted in tradition,

resumed by Vatican II: the Church as seed, sign and means of universal unity *(Lumen gentium,* nos. 1, 9 and 69). See our *This Church That I Love,* Dimension Books, 1968.

[7] See *Religion et institution,* in *Theologie d'aujourd'hui et de demain (Cogitatio fidei).* Paris, 1967, pp. 81 ff.

[8] Cf. R. Delaruelle, *La doctrine de la personne humaine, signe de contradiction entre le christianisme et le paganisme au 111ᵉ siècle,* in *Bull. Litter. ecclès.,* 53 (1952) 161-172.

[9] View of a cosmic hierarchy: saint Agustin, *De genesi ad litt.* VIII, 23, 44 (PL 34, 390): Denys, *De divinis nominibus* XI, 1, II. St. Thomas Aquinas, so original in his profound perception of the autonomy of the free person (see J. B. Metz), loves to situate moral and even spiritual realities within the frame of the general laws of the created cosmos: see, for example, I-II 87, I; III 7, 9. Bonaventure or Albert Magnus take a similar approach. We could cite texts and monographs. Let us note that the master-words like *iustitia* (Gregory VII), *rectitudo* (Anselm), *ordo* (throughout the 13th century), even *libertas,* involved a reference to a universal order: for each human being, his *libertas* consisted in actually occupying his exact place, and in the exercise therein of the duties and rights of his condition, etc.

[10] *Lumen gentium,* nos. 12 and 30; decree on the apostolate of the laity, nos. 3 and 30.

[11] We have had (and we still have) an overly clerical ecclesiology in which everything came from the clerics, everything was determined by them. Ed. LeRoy's observation, which we cited in *Lay people in the Church,* was hardly an exaggeration: "the simple faithful have the same part as the lambs at Candlemas: they are blessed and shorn." What was the place of charisms, the plurality of ministries in this Church without active participation? What did one do in this Church with the values of personal gifts and vocations, isolated in the domain of the "spiritual life"? Was the Christian freedom, of which St. Paul and St. Thomas Aquinas speak, always considered, always respected (see I. de La Potterie and S. Lyonnet, *La vie selon*

l'Esprit, condition du chrétien, Paris, Cerf, 1965)? Does an official document, before Vatican II, exist that talks about it? What was, what is still our pneumatology, that is to say, our consciousness of the action of the Holy Spirit, of the free grace of God, in His people and even in the world? It is true that on all these points, the *practice* was more positive than the theory. Nevertheless it was more bridled than excited by a theology that was fearful of everything which came from below, and of life itself. Today, we have H. Küng, *Structures of the Church* (Thomas Nelson and Sons, New York), K. Rahner *Elements dynamiques dans l'Eglise,* Paris, 1967, and Vatican II. The de-clericalization of our ecclesiology, however, is just managing to be outlined.

[12] To cite but one author we refer to Giles of Rome, *De potestate ecclesiastica* (published by R. Scholz, Weimar, 1929), I, 5; II, 5; III, 2.

[13] Cited by Chateaubriand in *Memoires d'Outre-tombe,* 3rd part, 2nd epoch, book IV, 8 (published by Centenaire, t. III, pp. 271-272.

[14] D. Dubarle, in *Un nouveau style d'obéissance,* Collection, *Problèmes de vie religieuse.* Paris, Cerf, 1968, pp. 13-14. We could set alongside them these observations of Fr. J. M. Le Blond, *Etudes,* July-August 1966, p. 104: "It is not surprising that authority is increasingly being conceived as a responsibility and as a function more than as a dignity, that it is taken first of all not as a 'right' that imposes duties but as a duty which, in order to be performed, entails rights and powers . . . That implies that authority appear then as founded, not upon the past and upon acquired situations, but upon the future and upon effectualness in consideration of the common good."

[15] We are thinking, for example, of an article such as that by Otto Ter Reegen, *Les droits des laïcs,* in *Concilium,* no. 38, 1968; pp. 19-30. Or even of certain demands set forth in January 1969 at the 3rd session of the Dutch pastoral Council.

[16] We cite this passage from the excellent article by P. H. Simon, *Contestation et culture (Le Monde,* July 27, 1968): "A

mixed pattern of simplified Marxism and falsified Freudianism is in the process of assuming the force of a dogma: namely that the disciple is alienated by the authority of the teacher as the son by the authority of the father. No doubt a danger exists: a certain fashion of stifling the son's consciousness under the apparatus of traditions and that of falsifying the pupil's mind by an inoculated dogmatism does, in fact, call the contestant reaction into being. But the distinction must be rigorously maintained, on the one hand, between the alienating power of the father and of the teacher and, on the other, the auxiliary power of the one and the other, the indispensable seminal action which they exercise on the plane of life and of culture. For it is not true that life and culture develop as if the individual owes nothing to his biological and social roots, as if he could enter into activity and into studies with his forces alone, furnished with a sufficient experience and an infused knowledge and, though still nescient, find himself in disputation on a footing of equality with those who have learned and constructed. Paternal or professorial authority does have this justification, I dare say this dignity: it protects and it informs . . ."

[17] J. P., in *Témoignage chrétien,* 14-11-1968.

[18] Ed. Schillebeeckx, *L'Eglise du Christ et l'homme d'aujourd'hui selon Vatican II.* Le Puy-Lyon, Mappus, 1965, pp. 122 ff.

[19] Cardinal Suenens, *La coresponsabilité dans l'Eglise d'aujourd'hui,* DDB 1968.

[20] See J. Ratzinger, *Frères dans le Christ.* Paris, Cerf, 1962.

[21] There is a tendency, at the present time, to lead all law back to a sacramental foundation. We do not believe that this is correct. Nevertheless it is necessary to pursue the research, felicitously begun, in order to disclose other sources of law than the will of the public authority: See for example, G. Lafont, *L'Esprit-Saint et le droit dans l'institution religieuse,* in *Supplément de la Vie spirituelle,* no. 82, September 1967.

[22] *La notion chrétiene d'autorité.* Paris, 1955 p. 34.

²³ II-III, q. 104, art. I and 4.

²⁴ In *L'Episcopat et l'Eglise universelle (Unam Sanctam,* 39). Paris, 1962, pp. 67 ff, as well as in *Pour une Eglise servante et pauvre,* Paris, 1963.

²⁵ Compare L. Lochet, in *Parole et Mission,* no. 36, January 1967 pp. 84 ff; Msgr. Marty, at the Symposium of Bishops of Europe, Noordwijkerhout, July 1967 (Cf. *Documentation catholique* 1967, col. 1773-1780.

²⁶ Compare on this point H. Bartoli and J. M. Domenach in *Esprit,* November 1954, for example p. 600.

²⁷ Pius XII already criticized it in his speech of November 2, 1954 (AAS, 1954, pp. 671, 673-674).

²⁸ See our article *Apostolicité de ministère et apostolicité de doctrine. Réaction protestante et tradition catholique,* in *Volk Gottes, Festgabe für Joseph Höfer.* 1967, pp. 84-111.

²⁹ On this practice of the epoch of the Church Fathers, see our study *Ordinations invitus, coactus, de l'Eglise antique au canon 214,* in *Revue des Sciences phil. théol.* 50 (1966), 169-197.

Chapter 6

¹ John A. T. Robinson, *But that I can't believe!* London, Collins (1965).

² Other examples and references can be found in our study *Langage des Spirituels et langage des Théologiens,* in *Situation et taches présentes de la Théologie,* Paris, Cerf, 1967.

Chapter 7

¹ *Considérations sur le système philosophique de M. de La Mennais.* Conclusion: *Oeuvres philosophiques et politiques.* Paris, Poussielgue, 1872, p. 163.